A BEGINNER'S GUIDE

Backyard Gardening
vegetables

EVERYTHING YOU NEED TO
KNOW ABOUT THE BASICS ON
PLANTING VEGETABLES ALL YEAR
ROUND. FROM PLANTING, TO
HARVESTING AND STORING

ELLE JOHN

TABLE OF CONTENTS

INTRODUCTION

Introduction

There are many reasons why you should consider cultivating a vegetable garden at home. The benefits of growing some of your vegetable intake yourself are many and varied. First off, you can be confident that they have been grown using responsible breeding, pest control, and fertilization (well, as long as you adhere to the highest standards in all these, of course).

Gardening is a relatively easy task when you know what you are doing. You may have a rough idea of the activities you will be engaged in; tilling, seeding, weeding, harvesting, and of course feasting on the fruits of your hard labors, but you will need to dig in deeper than that. There are more things to it than just getting your hands dirty or watering your succulent plants with a pink watering can and talking to them.

This book aims to give you a concise idea of the whole process of starting a vegetable garden, even in the limited space of your apartment. Among the issues that we will cover include:

- Picking out a garden space; determining the right space for your vegetable garden, working out the best way to organize your garden, and getting it ready for cultivation.

- Identifying the best vegetables to plant in your garden, keeping in mind that different types of vegetables require different weather conditions. In essence, plants for the summer, winter, spring, and autumn.

- The supplements your crops need to grow in a healthy and vigorous manner. These include water, fertilizers (organic preferred), and worms- yes, worms, those squiggly, slimy little crawlies that you probably fear may also come into play.

- Controlling pests is probably the most important aspect of the growing phase. If you don't control pests, they might decimate your whole crop. If you don't do it right, you may end up with vegetables that are not as healthy as you may (and should) want them to be.

- Storing your harvest. If you plan your garden well, supplement your crops properly, and control those bothersome pests as you should, you will end up with a bountiful   harvest. Too much in fact to eat it all straight from the garden- oops! But that should be a good thing. It means that you have become a master gardener. If you store your produce well, it also means that you will have more of those self-grown vegetables that you are 100% sure about.

Now gardening is not exactly a walk in the park. It will take up quite a lot of your time and energies. It will also be a while before the fruits of all your labors manifest. But you can be sure that you will have quite a lot of fun setting up your vegetable garden, and what's more, nothing quite matches up to the joy you will get when you finally get a taste of vegetables from your own garden.

So roll up those sleeves, dig in, and let's get to work! See what I did there? ☺☺☺

CHAPTER 1
WHAT IS YOUR 'WHY'?

- ## <u>Pros and Cons</u>

You can get vegetables from pretty much any grocery store. You can order from any of a dozen online stores and have fresh vegetables delivered to your house in less than one hour. So why should you get your hands dirty growing your own vegetables?

Pros

The first reason to consider is your own health. When you grow your own vegetables, you will obviously end up eating more of them. The commitment and dedication you show to your garden also increases your commitment to healthy living. An article published in the *Journal of American Diabetic Association* indicated that families ate more organic foods (especially fruits and vegetables) when there was the constant reminder of the same in the form of a backyard garden. And growing your own vegetables could literally save your life. Your vegetable   garden allows you to avoid such food-borne illnesses like E. coli and salmonella, the former of which has taken lives and sickened many more as recently as 2006. These illnesses are spread to the consumer through inputs like manure used in large scale farms to supply mass markets with vegetables.

Besides the health benefits, having a vegetable garden right in your backyard ensures that you always get your vegetables farm fresh. And because you do the picking yourself, you can be sure that the "farm fresh" is not just a marketing gimmick. So if you like the idea of savoring your vegetables then crisp and juicy, garden-fresh vegetables, grown by your own hand, is the way to go. And the cost of all this awesomeness is much lower than you would think. The National Gardening Association estimates a return of about ten times the cost of cultivating a vegetable garden, which comes in at about $70. So what you are looking at is a great saving on your groceries budget for greater benefits than that $700 would ever get you.

Apart from the health and financial considerations, other reasons to start a vegetable garden is actually physical activity. Gardening is a rather labor-intensive activity, especially when you have a larger patch to cultivate. You will need to stretch across your vegetable bed, work with your hands, and walk around for hours on end tending to each crop. Studies have shown that up to 400 calories are burned up when you engage in moderate gardening activities like weeding by hand or watering. More calories are burned out when you do more tasking activities like tilling. A nice, long session of working in your garden is as good as a run or a walk. Better even, because you will get some juicy vegetables to boost your health even further in just a couple of weeks or months!

The physical benefits of gardening go far beyond burning a few calories. The act of farming vegetables can be very calming, therapeutic even. For you, a garden can be something through which to reconnect with nature. Nothing beats the wonder of watching as the seeds you put under the ground sprout and start to grow and following their progress as they bloom, flower, and produce the very vegetable you love. For your kid, a garden could be a way to build nurturing, responsible character. The University of Illinois at Urbana-Champaign has actually uncovered evidence that point to gardening as a way to help kids with Attention Deficit Hyperactivity Disorder (ADHD).

I know what you must be thinking. "It's all great that gardening will be a great opportunity to nurture kids into conscientious adults later on in life, but am I supposed to just let them loose on my garden?" And the answer is, "of course not!" And this answer brings us to the other reason why you should consider cultivating a vegetable garden. A garden allows for socialization and bonding, whether it is on the dinner table or at the garden where vegetables are tended to and nurtured. While you water, weed, or add fertilizer to your plants together with your daughter, son, nephew, niece, or any other person- young or grown- your connection with them is boosted in a way few other activities can afford you.

Incorporating your garden into available space can also be a very rewarding idea. Depending on the space you have, you may consider adding a bench in the midst of the garden to create a soothing ambiance, some place to rewind after a long week and just breathe the purified air. A few minutes spent in the picture-perfect space of a well-organized garden is just the thing your psyche needs to stay sharp. Whether you prefer to do it on the garden bench (just taking in the sights) or with a tool at hand, gardening can be a great way to decompress and meditate.

Another reason to consider taking up gardening is for mother earth. It may not be much, but taking the incentive to produce your own vegetables in a clean and environmentally friendly way goes a long way in reducing the carbon footprint associated with the American dinner table and general eating habits. By producing your vegetables yourself, you reduce the overall emissions from mass production farms, factories, storage, and transportation. Over a few years, who knows, your impact may actually be felt by the whole world!

Gardening makes you happy. It takes you back to those childhood days when you were intrigued with dirt, but this time, there is no one to stop you from indulging in this earthy pleasure. Scientists have found evidence that point to a linkage between dirt and the brain's serotonin-releasing neurons. The link creates the same kind of reaction that antidepressants are designed to induce in the brain. And sure you might find it difficult to believe this while engaging in the backbreaking work of tilling your garden patch, but you wait until those shoots break the soil surface and you will know real joy.

Cons

Whatever it might look like, gardening is not all sunshine and daisies. Well, actually it could be a little of that if you planted a few daisies in your vegetable patch to cheer things up;   The point is, however beneficial gardening might be, there is a downside to it too.

The first difficulty in starting a vegetable garden is the time factor. You will find that your garden requires constant attention, work, and attending to from tilling to harvesting. If you are not capable of investing a fixed amount of time every week to tend to the current needs of your garden, you will find it difficult to keep up with the work. Even worse, your garden might end up falling by the wayside. If you want to be depressed really quick, just imagine a vegetable patch that has been overrun by weeds; the crops you have nurtured for so long choked   out and probably killed off. If your job requires you to put in the hours or you travel for work a lot, a garden may be too much of a hassle for you. The only way you'd make it work then would be if you can get family members to help out or if you joined a communal garden. That way, you can work on the garden when you can and count on the others to keep it going whenever you can't personally see to it.

Another opportunity cost for starting a garden is vacationing. With the growing season, even for the fastest-growing vegetables, spanning a few months it would be hard to leave your home at the spur of the moment, especially for long periods of time. Again, you can overcome this huddle by planning well in advance and having a strong support group of neighbors, friends, or family who can watch your garden in your absence.

Starting a vegetable garden is also quite costly. Depending on where you live, you may have to have some vegetable beds made, procure some soil to grow your vegetables in, buy the tools you will need to start cultivating, buy seeds, fertilizers, pesticides, and a myriad of other expenses. Before you can get to that level of spending ten times less in produce in comparison to in farm inputs   , you will need to put in a good deal of capital into the garden. You may also expect some of your utility bills like water to grow considerably with the garden in need of constant watering.

The usual way for a family to deck out the backyard is to create a play and entertainment area for the whole family. The garden competes for space with these more conventional needs and you will have to forego a bit of each to balance everything out. Space-saving gardening practices like trellises for climbing vegetables and use of vertical spaces can maximize your garden space while limiting the amount of space appropriated from play and entertainment. By incorporating gardening with entertainment and play to save space, you can rest assured that someone will always be keeping an eye out for your vegetable patch even when they didn't initially intend to do so. The one big risk to this whole arrangement is that your crops may get trampled on if (or, let's face it, when) play gets out of hand.

Finally, I mentioned above that gardening is a physically exerting activity. The digging, stooping, bending, and hauling of heavy supplies could damage your joints. These activities may potentially be even more dangerous if your garden is a rooftop affair and your building has no lift. Hauling 50 pounds of manure up five or more flights of stairs might be very tedious indeed. And of course the bigger your garden is the greater the strain it will put on you. Consider paying someone to do the harder stuff like carrying and focus on the easier activities. And take breaks; gardening is supposed to be fun, not a punishment.

So there you have it; all the reasons to start a vegetable garden and all the sacrifices you will have to pay to keep it going. Needless to say, the pros far outweigh the cons. You can always find a workaround for every challenge. And in the case of gardening, the workaround often makes it all the more rewarding.

CHAPTER 2
YOUR GARDEN TERRITORY

Now that you have decided to start growing your own vegetables, let's get to the basics of this noble undertaking. Don't let the backyard in the title of this book fool you. You can start a vegetable garden even in the open space of your apartment building if you have one. If your balcony is big enough, it can provide you with a respectable amount of space to start your own vegetable garden.

Your garden territory is any space available to you with access to direct sunshine in which a few vegetables can be grown. The truth is, whether you live in the suburbs where yards are large and green, or you live in an apartment in the middle of town, you can engage in gardening if you are really determined. Of course in an apartment building you will have to find out if your lease agreement allows for such activities and bring up your own soil, taking care to leave no lasting damage to the floors or the walls, but it can be done. In the next chapter, we will look at plant beds as an alternative to on-the-ground planting. They can be very useful for you as an apartment dweller.

For homeowners with a grassy yard, gardening is a matter of taking a hoe to the ground and turning the earth to make a garden, but for anyone living in vertical housing (owned, leased, or rented) creating a garden requires greater effort, including buying the soil to plant on; you know, because the linoleum floors of your house are not conducive for plant growth. But the first thing you need to do is select the site for your garden. Here are a few things that influence your selection of the right site to locate your garden   :

- **<u>Sunlight:</u>**   vegetables require a minimum of 6 hours direct sunlight every day. You may compensate with special lighting in a greenhouse, but that is quite an expensive alternative and not well  suited for small-scale gardening. Avoid shaded areas of your backyard. If none exist, consider creating some by, say, pruning any trees that might be blocking the sun from reaching the ground.

- **<u>Drainage:</u>** your vegetables will need water to grow, but you should know that too much water is harmful to their health. The location for your garden must not be soggy ground or else your vegetables will grow very poorly

- **<u>Water supply:</u>** if you are lucky enough to live in a place where crops can grow all year round under normal circumstances, then you need not worry about water supply. If, on the other hand your location experiences periods of dry weather, ensuring that your garden is in close proximity to a water tap might save you a lot of work transporting it to the garden.

There are two ways to start a vegetable garden. You can either till the ground in your backyard to create a plantable plot of land, or you can set up some plant beds with your choice of soil. If you are planting in  natural ground as opposed to the plant bed, something to look out for is weed growth. Those sections of your backyard that are overgrown with weeds are obviously very fertile and ideal is very likely to be barren.

 DETERMINING YOUR SPACE SIZE

The space you dedicate to your vegetable garden is determined by a few factors like available open spaces where you live, time, and the types of vegetables you'd like to plant.

Depending on where you live, your garden size can either be huge or tiny. If you are an apartment dweller planting in your balcony or the rooftop of your apartment building, you may be looking at a plot measuring 10 feet by 10 feet or less. This is also a great size for a beginner; a place where you can learn all about gardening firsthand with less risk of loss.

According to the National Gardening Association, the standard garden space of 100 square feet is required to grow vegetables for one person per season.

If the small allotment of 10*10 feet is all you can muster, even after you have become a master gardener and you are looking for more, then you may look into vertical expansion. As long as you space your rows well, it is possible to maximize space use by having more than one level of crops. This increases your yield per unit foot and assures you greater yield than the simple one-level mode of gardening ground-use.

Gardening in an apartment building may be a little difficult. You will be facing stiff competition from your fellow tenants for any public space that would be suitable for a vegetable garden. Neither can you be sure that everyone else will treat your crops with the same reverence you do.

If you live in a standalone building with your own open space, front, or back yard, then you have somewhat of an advantage over the apartment dweller. For one, you don't need to ask for permission from the landlord to start a garden. You also have more space to yourself, unlike the apartment where objections may be raised to appropriating common areas for a vegetable garden.

With the luxury of space, you can choose to cultivate a larger portion of your garden: up to 400 sq. ft. The vegetables harvested from a 400 sq. ft garden can comfortably feed 4 for a whole summer. Your choice of vegetables to plant is also much better with a larger garden as you can plant such space-demanding crops like watermelons and pumpkins.

A garden measuring 10 feet by 10 feet is relatively easy to cultivate. You can do it comfortably in your off-work hours and the weekends. However, anything bigger could prove to be too much of a hassle. Depending on the amount of time you can free up from the rest of your weekly activities, add to the size of your garden if the space is available.

Remote work gives you a lot more time at home. The morning and evening commute and those downturns that would otherwise have been used gossiping in the office can go towards your garden. The size of your garden can be bigger without compromising your ability to work on it. If you are a stay-at-home spouse, on the other hand, then you can start a garden of whatever size available. With all the time open for exploration, starting a vegetable garden would be a great way to occupy your time. And what's more, the vegetables supplementing your family's food budget will go a long way in making you feel like you are contributing more to the upkeep of the whole family.

Different vegetables require different space allocation. Later in this book, we will discuss the area each type of vegetable requires to grow well. In essence, certain vegetables require much room- as much as 3 feet apart- which makes it a little harder to plant them in constricted spaces. If you have already made up your mind what to plant, consider how much space it will require to produce enough (or at least sufficient) produce for your needs. More   than you can eat will probably lead to wastage and too little is likely to make you feel like you wasted a lot of your time for no tangible results.

DESIGNING YOUR GARDEN

After taking care of the basics (area available, time you have to work on your garden, and space requirements for your preferred vegetable if you have one), it is time now to get into the technicalities. You need to work out the area of your backyard, rooftop, balcony, or patio that you will use for gardening. The best idea is to make a detailed plan, marking out your space allocation   on your computer or a sketch pad with accurate measurements. This way, you can budget for the raw materials you will need to get the garden up and running.

Making a plan beforehand allows you to make the most efficient use of the space available to you. With a full understanding of the growing patterns of different types of vegetables, you can plan for the climbers nearer to the fence, and fast-maturing ones between larger ones because they will soon be tall enough to compete for light anyways. A plan also allows you to arrange everything in a way that gradually frees up space as vegetables mature and leave the garden when harvesting time comes.

A garden design also gives you the chance to figure out how to take care of storage for the garden tools and the harvest. With enough space and security outside, you can have a tool chest to keep your shovels, hoes, gloves, watering cans, etc. Just be careful that the storage area is well guarded from the elements because you don't want your iron implements rusting.

Also, when budgeting for space, leave enough room all around for you to maneuver as you plant, weed, water, apply pesticides, and harvest. About a foot all-round is the standard garden path, so be sure to account for it.

VERTICAL GARDEN

Now the ultimate design in vegetable gardening is the vertical garden. It is made possible by the fact that crops generally don't need all the soil in the garden to grow. Instead, a small section of earth around the plant nourishes it with water, nutrients, and provides it with anchorage. Vertical gardening provides just the necessary of earth around the plant for these basic needs, providing you with great economy on water and fertilizer use as well as reducing the space that weeds can take up.

Vertical gardening is especially useful for apartment dwellers with limited space. You can use specially designed troughs or take just any container and fill it with soil to create a growing base for your crops. The depth of your container is essential. You need it to be deep enough to facilitate root development but also to be economical in the space it takes up and the amount of soil that you need to fill it up. In this style of gardening, you can use shelves, hanging baskets, or trellises.

Shelves are attached to a wall or supported by pillars to provide a raised oblong ground where you can grow a row of vegetables much like you would grow them on the ground. The positioning of your shelves is   critical because it has to be done in such a way that they don't block access to sunshine by other crops on your garden.

Drainage in shelves is accomplished by leaving small slats at the bottom to allow excess water to seep through and also promote better circulation of air in your soil.

Standalone containers are the next big thing in vertical gardening. With standalone containers, a single plant goes into the jar. You can use an empty jar, a bucket, or a basket, making sure to make drainage holes at the bottom of the first two to ensure that excess water drains through and at the sides to promote airflow. Baskets are naturally drained and aerated, so you don't have to worry about making holes in them.

Trellises do not provide you with extra space to plant your crops. Instead, they allow you to take maximum use of available vertical space by directing vine crops upwards instead of laterally. This takes much less space and has the added advantage of enhancing the aesthetic appeal of your garden.

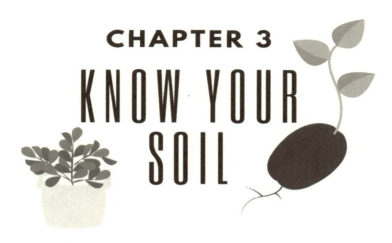

CHAPTER 3
KNOW YOUR SOIL

Gardening is all about knowing the soil on which you plant. Without a basic understanding of soil types, it is unlikely that you will choose the best quality soil for the kind of vegetables you have in mind. Planting in the wrong type of soil is worse than not planting at all. You could end up seeing your hard work go down the drain.

The types

Soils fall under 6 categories namely   sand, clay, loam, chalk, peat, and silt. These six soil types have different features and carry different percentages of organic life, soil air, and water. As such, each soil is well suited for the growth of a particular type of vegetables as discussed below.

Sandy soil

Sand is a very airy type of soil that is coarse, loosely packed, and light. Due to the numerous air spaces sandy soil contains, water runs through it very fast. The poor water retention

means that sandy soils heat up quicker than other soils in summer time and thus require   more watering to keep the plant nourished with water. In the rainier seasons, this excellent drainage quality causes sandy soils to quickly lose their nutrients to leaching   .

To improve the nutritional value of sandy soils, it is advised that you add organic fertilizers or organic additives like kelp meal, greensand, and glacial rock dust. These supplements provide sandy soil with the minerals required to sustain plant life. To retain water, mulching is a great idea for preventing evaporation. Vegetables that do well in sandy soils include the root family of potatoes, parsnips, and carrots. The loose compaction of sandy soil allows these vegetables to grow uninhibited.

Clay soil

Clayey soils are compact and sticky in wet weather and hard as rock in dry seasons. While its drainage qualities are at the opposite end of the spectrum from sand (it retains all the water and  lets nothing through) it is still considered a poorly drained soil. The reason clay retains all its water is because the soil contains very few air spaces. While this particular type of soil is extremely nutritional, the poor drainage and stickiness makes it extremely hard to cultivate .

Vegetables with quick maturity should definitely be kept off the clay soils. The lumpiness will make it hard for them to send out roots quickly enough. However, the soil can be very good for growing crops in the summer because it does not lose its soil water as fast as sandy soils. Any water applied to the garden patch will thus last a long time and allow your vegetables to grow vigorously. Due to its high nutrient value, clay only needs aeration, which may be provided by mixing it up with organic substances like wood chips, mulch, or compost .

Loam soil

Loam is a natural blend of clay and sandy soils. As such, it takes the middle ground of the qualities of these two soils. Loam has a fine texture and is rather lumpy, drains well but does not lose all water, and contains a median amount of air. The nutritional value of loam soil is also very good, it doesn't dry up too fast in the summer, or hold excessive water in winter. Loamy soils are the most common soil types and they are used extensively in lawns and gardens everywhere. Loam is naturally productive because it maintains a balance that sand and clay simply do not.

Just like any soil, loam needs replenishment from time to time, especially with organic matter to enhance its microbe properties. As a gardening soil, loam is very well suited to pretty much any vegetable, but climbers in particular demand this type of soil as it allows them to get anchorage to spread their vines and also enough mineral sustenance for their never-ending growth. This productive nature of loam soils also means that pests and crop diseases can thrive in them after a while, so be sure to practice crop rotation. To ensure the continued vitality of your loam soil, add compost, mulch, and organic fertilizers to avoid depletion.

Chalk soil

Chalk is the bigger brother to sand. It has huge grains that drain freely and is very alkaline. pH is something to be very concerned about with chalky soils and if you don't bring it down to more acceptable levels, your crops will become stunted and unproductive. Use chalk soil in your garden to grow cabbages, sweet corn, spinach, and beetroots. These grow very well in properly moderated chalky soils.

Peat

Peat is thus named for containing a high percentage of dead plants. The soil is dark, rather spongy, and quite damp. Despite the high content of decomposing matter,

peat is very low in nutritional matter. But it can hold a large amount of water and heat up quick during summer, though not quite as fast as your sandy soils. Unlike clay, peat can be drained by digging drainage channels to allow water to seep through.

Decomposing organic matter raise the acidity of the soil, which means that bases like lime can be great for balancing it out. Vegetables that do well in peat include legumes, brassicas, salads, and root vegetables.

Silt

Silt is a rich agricultural soil that only lacks in drainage. As the product of leached and eroded soils, silt contains a lot of nutrients, but it's fine grains packs together and makes aeration rather difficult. This is easily fixed with a good  measure of compost and the resulting soil is suitable for growing pretty much any type of vegetable. Just be sure to monitor the soil's properties and add compost when the soil's structure deteriorates.

 ## ASSESSING YOUR SOIL

Now, you know every type of soil that you will find out there, and you also have a good clue what to do to improve the quality of each type. You still need to learn how to figure out the type of soil that you have in your garden.

To find out what types of soil you have in your garden, select a few random spots in your garden and remove the top level, including any grass or plants. DO NOT take a soil sample in any spots that do not bear close resemblance to the rest of the garden- under trees, for example. With the top level gone, dig about 6 inches into the ground and scoop out some soil into a container. A trowel-full will be enough for this exercise. Repeat this process with a few other spots until you have a reasonable amount.

Compare your soil with the description given above of different soil types. The senses are your closest ally in discovering just what type of soil you have in your garden. The texture, color, and smell all tell a story about your soil. Earthy smells indicate fertility and a soil rich in microorganisms, odors point toward anaerobic matter and lack of air. Dark soils tend to have more organic matter while light ones are just barren. On texture, a grating feel indicates large granules of the sandy and chalky family while softer and silkier textures belong to the clay and silt soil types.

For a more scientific way of assessing your soil type, follow the following process with the soil you dug up for the process above.

- Add a small amount of soil into a clear jar and fill with water then shake vigorously. Leave the jar unshaken for 24 hours then measure the layers visible inside. Sand is what settles at the bottom, followed by silt, clay, and then organic matter. An ideal loam has 45%, 25% 25%, and 5% of these components respectively. More than 60% of sand indicates sandy soil and less than 40% is for clayey types. Peat will have as much as 20% organic matter. You can then follow the remedies given above for these less productive soil types.

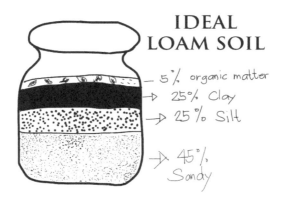

IDEAL LOAM SOIL
- 5% organic matter
- 25% Clay
- 25% Silt
- 45% Sandy

PLANT BEDS

If you find that your soil is bad and you don't want to take a chance with fixing it yourself or contracting an agricultural professional to do it for you, then you should consider making a plant bed. A plant bed saves you the hassle of hauling burrows of compost into your garden- probably getting it wrong over and over again- and takes you right into the jackpot. Buy professionally mixed soil, make a trough to pour it into, and viola-a perfect blend of sandy, silt, clay, and organic matter for the ideal gardening experience.

Plant beds are also ideal because they allow for small-space gardening practices like vertical support and sequential planting because you don't need necessarily need to give the soil time to recover lost minerals. Organic matter added to a plant bed soil after harvesting can be used in the very next planting season with no problem at all. And because the good quality soil in plant beds allows for denser planting, weeds have little room to grow and bother you. Another advantage of plant beds is that they are higher than the ground. Thus you bend down less to work on them, meaning that you don't get quite as tired.

Raised beds can be bought in gardener supply stores in any town. They are made out of different materials, including aluminum, timber, and concrete. The latter lasts a long time but is very heavy to transport, but wood and aluminum combined make a great plant bed.

Ideal depth for plant beds is about one foot to ensure that tap roots do not encounter bad soils underneath if you are placing it on your poor soil. For apartment dwellers with concrete as the base for their plant beds and needing to avoid destroying the floors, a plant bed with a covered floor should be used. Ensure that the bed is slightly slanted to allow excess water to flow off and collect it otherwise it could grow soggy at the bottom.

The top dimensions of your plant bed can be as small or as

big as you would like them to be. The good aspect of this is that you are the boss here. Whatever you say goes. However if you will not be climbing on top of the plant bed to do your weeding and watering and other operations, keep the width at about five feet for a plant bed with a path on both sides and around three feet if the path is at one side only. You should be able to reach every part of the plant bed without any strain.

CHAPTER 4
KNOW YOUR WEATHER

The atmospheric condition of a place- wind, humidity, sunshine, temperature, and precipitation- affects crops in very many ways. Higher atmospheric temperatures cause faster growth of plants, but after a certain level, rising temperatures are detrimental to the plant and will actually cause stunted growth brought about by excessive moisture loss. The amount of heat inside the soil also affects plant growth. Seed germination is especially vulnerable to soil temperatures. Colder temperatures may cause very slow germination as well as growth as plants hoard energy while higher temperatures may kill plant cells and cause the plant to wilt and die off. Wind accelerates water loss to the environment, sunshine increases the processing of food by the plant, but past a certain point it has the same effects as temperature.

The weather can either be your friend or your bitter foe in your bid to start the perfect all-year garden. The four seasons and their corresponding differences in weather conditions make it rather difficult to grow annual crops that require certain fixed growth conditions. The alternative therefore becomes to grow short period crops in the existing conditions, harvest them when conditions no longer favor their growth, and plant another type of vegetable suited to the new conditions.

The Department of Agriculture releases the USDA Plant Hardiness Zone Map to indicate the types of crops that grow well in certain regions at certain times of the year. You can actually access this database and find out what vegetables are suited to the existing conditions of your ZIP code at any time of the year. This list is current to the year 2012 when it was last updated. The USDA Plant Hardiness Zone gives recommendations based on information like last and first frost dates for the winter season; dates that you should familiarize yourself with, now that you are becoming invested in an activity that depends of weather patterns. If you cannot find out these details from gardening websites in your area or other sources, try and acquaint yourself with a few gardeners. They are most likely to have recorded these dates.

Going forward, it is important that you start a weather diary, recording changing weather patterns like first rain, last rain, first and last snow, and other pertinent details about the weather in your city of residence. Institutions like garden.org are also very valuable in understanding weather patterns and their effects on a crop cycle. Pay close attention to growth seasons, because they are now a part of your life. So what are they, really?

The growth season is the duration when a region has

suitable weather conditions to grow a certain crop. Weather conditions change throughout the year and different plants have different requirements for growth. Putting these two factors into consideration, you will realize that there is always a crop that requires the prevailing weather conditions at any one time. Like I mentioned above, the trick is in finding the right crop for every season.

The growing season of most vegetables starts in spring and ends between early summer and late winter. The overwhelming majority take a month to four months to reach maturity, which means that they are out of   the garden in the fall. Plants like   stem vegetables are better suited to the cool of fall but need to be out of   the garden in early winter.

Very few crops can survive the cold temperatures of winter and those that do need to be planted earlier. They include asparagus (as a perennial crop, it grows around the year and produces tender, juicy stalks when harvested in winter), kale, and perpetual spinach which grow right through the cold, developing new leaves   when the mature ones are harvested, even in winter. All these crops do well when   planted in the fall before   encountering the winter chill in the later stages of their growth. The winter squash is almost the only crop that starts its life   in the winter.

Summer vegetables include cinnamon, summer squash, some plant stems in the late weeks, and a few cruciferous vegetables like the kohlrabi and the pak choi.

Root vegetables grow well when planted in the fall or spring. Their tolerance to cold allows them to grow through the bitter frost of winter.

With a good understanding of weather patterns and the suitability of different vegetables to varying weather conditions, you are assured of maintaining a healthy garden all through the year. But keep in mind that spring is the most suitable season to grow vegetables, so make arrangements to free up as much of the garden as you can to plant the fast-growing, bountiful   harvest vegetable(s) of your choice in time.

CHAPTER 5
ESSENTIAL GARDEN TOOLS

Your garden tools are to you what a gun and ammo are to a soldier: vital. Without the right tools, neither the soldier nor the gardener can do their work right. There is always a tool for every gardening activity and your understanding of the use of every implement will actually be critical to the liveliness of your vegetable garden and ultimately, the quantity and quality of vegetables you will harvest in the end.

The secret in buying gardening tools is to go for quality over price. If you buy the right quality tools, then with good maintenance they could last you a few decades. Cheap tools will just break in your hands over and over again, causing you no little amount of grief and a fortune in replacing them. Look at the tools as an investment in everything good about gardening; your spiritual and physical wellbeing, a healthier diet, better social connections, doing your bit in saving mother earth from the tide of global warming.

So what exactly determines if a tool is considered good or bad? First off, look at the handle. You will be working with the tool for a long time; holding it in your hand and probably doing some effortful digging so it has got to fit right in your hands and not cause too much friction lest your hands become permanently covered in blisters. Second, the harmony between the tool and the handle used to wield it is very important. A handle that has been attached to the tool   with screws, rivets, or a close fit, is weaker than one that is part of the tool.

Another important thing to check off in a tool is the size and how suitable it is for you. Whether it is a fork, a hoe, or a spade, you need it to be the right size for YOU or one or two things will happen. One, you may have to bend a long way to use it if it is too short, or it will be too big and very uncomfortable to use. An easy way to check for the right size is to place it on the ground. The tip of the handle ought to reach your elbow at resting pose.

Now let's look at those tools that you definitely have to own as you begin your gardening journey.

The hoe

The gardening hoe comes in handy at all processes of gardening, but more in some than others. You definitely need a hoe to plow the ground and turn over the soil to ready it for harvesting and also to dig holes for seedlings. The hoe is also great for removing weeds from your garden.

The typical hoe consists of a wide 6-inch steel sharp edge well suited for pretty much every farming operation that involves turning over the soil in your garden. Other types of hoes include the collinear hoe that is more tapered out, making it ideal for weeding in dense vegetation and narrow spots.

As stated above, the handle is the most important part of your tool because it directly affects your ability to work. With the garden hoe, a wooden handle is ideal because it remains firm in your grasp even when you sweat during hot weather. A metallic handle is also more likely to cause blistering in your hands because it absorbs a lot of heat. The handle and blade combination is the most common form of hoe construction. It is done by simply fitting the blade over the handle. This design means that your blade is likely to keep sliding back and forth, a very uncomfortable and rather annoying thing to have to put up with. A garden hoe should ideally be an all-in-one tool, but since that would mean having a metallic handle, consider instead a hoe that contains a very firm screw joining the blade and the tool together.

The garden fork

Every garden needs two types of fork; a large one for digging and a smaller cottage fork that is used for more delicate gardening operations. The fork is a very dynamic implement. The thin long blades penetrate 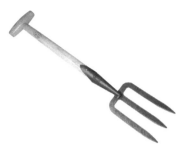 deep into the ground to allow you to turn sods of soil over in preparation for planting. It also comes in handy when turning your compost heaps over. Finally, the fork is the ideal tool for harvesting potatoes. Its thin long blades reduce the chances of you driving a blade through the potatoes, a problem that is very rife with spades and hoes.

The cottage fork comes in handy in separating   huge plants like   agapanthus and dahlias to divide them and create new plantings. The cottage fork is also preferable for smaller gardens because it is easier to wield and, anyway, using the larger fork for a raised 3-   feet wide plant bed is a bit of overkill.

Unlike hoes, forks come fully assembled in industrial grades, mostly with a plastic gripping point and plastic-covered handle for better ergonomic quality. When selecting one, pick one that is made out of one steel piece from the handle to the tip of the blades. Middle blades that have been welded into the rest of the fork tend to be very susceptible to breakage. They may come off sometime down the line. The blades should also ideally be diamond-tipped to ensure greater strength in piercing through any kind of garden soil.

The spade

The spade is perhaps the most versatile (in design) garden tool. There are long and short handled square- bladed spades, short handled spades, heart-shaped spades; you  name any shape and perhaps there are three varieties of spades available for it. Some gardeners argue that a spade is not necessary, but it is indeed very useful around the garden. A spade gives you greater control of the edges of your vegetable patch, allowing you to straighten out those edges that the hoe left uneven. Any shovel with a pointy edge comes in handy when opening sacks of pretty much any supply for your garden, from soil to fertilizers. A spade also comes in handy when you are adding compost into the soil.

There are two essential sizes of a garden spade; the digging spade (approximate measurements of 11 inches by 12 inches) and the cottage one that spans 9 by 6 inches. The thinner blade allows maneuverability in tight spaces. As far as the things to look for before buying, the spade is essentially a fork with the blades filled out. You should follow the same procedure of choosing the blades and deciding what design to buy as the steps described for the garden fork above.

The rake

Depending on where you live, you may need one or two garden rakes. There is the landscape rake for creating a flat surface to plant new gardens, seedling beds, and flower beds; and the lawn rake that is effective for use in gathering leaves and other vegetation like mowed grass which are great materials for compost heaps.

The lawn rake has a plastic head with elongated flexible spikes often made from plastic. Lawn rakes with metal spikes are equipped with a   n adjusting device to allow for alterations to the tension when you rake out different materials from different surfaces. This particular tool is only useful if you live in a house that has a lawn with tree cover and thus a generous fall of leaves.

The landscape rake is the more universal gardening scraping tool; a more robust set of spikes allows you to move soil about more easily. The spikes are often metallic or hard plastic to extend its durability. With dimensions of about 14 inches, the head has two sides to it; one that digs into the surface to improve aeration for the patch of land you are working on, and another side to smooth it over. Handles are wooden, between 4 and 6 feet long (some steel handles have an adjustable length) and very firmly affixed to the head.

Wheelbarrow

A wheelbarrow is a tool that a vegetable garden and pretty much any garden can't do without. The barrow helps you cart those heavy garden supplies from one place to the other, including the fertilizers, compost, soil, and when it is plentiful enough, even the produce you harvest from your garden. Only the metal garden wheelbarrow is worth considering. Those plastic and canvas types will be a pain later on; you are better off keeping off them even though they cost much less.

The trowel and mini forks

These nifty little handheld tools are pretty indispensable for smaller gardens, especially plant beds. Since you most likely won't be climbing onto the plant bed, the trowel becomes pretty much like your handheld hoe and spade combination. The mini-fork is

also indispensable for loosening the soil, digging out planting holes, and removing tougher weed like dandelions. For these smaller tools, the grip in your hands must be just right, with no exposed screws that might be uncomfortable over a long time.

The hose pipe

Watering the garden is essential to keep your crops robust during the rainy season. However, be careful because not all vegetables take well to water on the leaves. Some, like potatoes, develop blight when water settles on them for long. On these, subtler methods of watering –like the watering can- will be needed. Do not buy a vinyl hose; it kinks up and stops the flow of water very often, especially if the distance from the tap to the garden is big. Also, go for one with washers and brass fittings as it is more reliable and lasts a long time.

The watering can

Mentioned above as the alternative to the hose pipe, the watering can is a more primitive way of transporting water from the source to the plants that need it. The bucket is rather ineffective because it requires filling up every few minutes as the water

empties out. Pick a screw-on sprinkler head rather than the one that just fits on the spout   to prevent water from escaping through. A special sprinkler head with an oval rose is used to water young shoots.

Others

Apart from these must-haves, there are tools that you might be able to substitute with stuff from your house but are still vital for your gardening activities.

- ***Knee pads and gardening stools;*** these are the tools that allow you to use different poses like kneeling and sitting in the garden without dirtying your clothes.

- ***Buckets;*** pails come in handy in an assortment of activities like moving fertilizers, soil, produce, hand tools, water, seeds, and pretty much any little objects that goes into the maintenance of a garden. You may opt for your own household buckets, but it is much better to have a metallic one specifically for the garden.

- ***Baskets;*** while the bucket may be used to carry some vegetables, there are specially designed tools for that- the basket family. These include wicker harvest baskets, wooden trugs, and wire hods. These are more fashionable for moving vegetables to the kitchen than any other tool you could muster for the job.

CHAPTER 6
PREPARING YOUR CROPS

The varieties of vegetables that exist are too many to count. However, they all fall under five families, namely cruciferous, cucurbit, alliums, edible roots, and plant stem vegetables. The different types of vegetables have the same nutritional properties. Their cultivation is also done in a similar manner.

Cruciferous Vegetables

The cruciferous vegetable (*also Brassica vegetables) are super foods that bring great value to the vegetable garden and the dinner table. Vegetables in the cruciferous family are also some of the most delicious you will ever eat. They contain vitamins A, C, E, iron, potassium , calcium, and folic acid; all critical to the well-being of the human body. Some of the health benefits of brassicas include boosting eyesight, regulating the inflammatory system, and preventing strokes and some types of cancers. Most of the vegetables in this family are perfect for salads. They include; kohlrabi, kales, cabbages, broccoli, and pak choi.

Cruciferous vegetables require slightly alkaline soils with a perfect balance of nitrogen, potassium, and phosphate. One of the means of achieving this balance of alkalinity and provide nutrients at the same time is to add manure during fall, but since manure alone creates an acidic environment that is totally unsuitable for the growth of cruciferous vegetables, farmers cover it up with lime to maintain the slight acidity they require for proper growth. The alternative, and the method you should use in growing these wonder foods, is to incorporate a rotational mode of crop planting by having legumes in the garden before planting time for your cruciferous vegetables. The nitrogen-rich roots of legumes are left in the ground to decompose and release their nitrogen in the soil. Bone meal is then mixed into the soil to provide the phosphorous the plants need. To raise potassium levels, wood ash is added to the soil. Wood ash has the added advantage of making the soil more alkaline, which is conducive for cruciferous vegetables.

Later on, a nitrogen supplement   is added directly into the soil or liquid feed is applied at the base of each the vegetable stem every week. The liquid state makes it easier for the plant to absorb the nitrogen faster. A perfect organic nitrogen supplement is the stinging nettle plant. Stored in water and left to ferment for a month, the plant produces such a concentrated nitrogenous liquid that it can be diluted 10:1 and still be effective. Of course, the leftover   leaves are perfect additions to the compost pit. An alternative to this rather time-   consuming supplement is chicken droppings or blood meal, both of which may be bought at gardening supply shops anywhere.

Vegetables of the cruciferous family tend to be annual, lasting from late spring to early spring the next year in the garden. However, some like the pak choi has a shorter duration of growth- from late summer to early fall. For the vegetables that have a longer duration, the long span of growth allows the plant to accumulate the foods that go into making it a juicy, nutritious vegetable, but it also calls for you as the gardener to consider weather changes and how they are likely to affect the crop. And since they grow to a large size with proper nourishment, cruciferous vegetables require firm soils for proper anchorage. You should not dig out your garden before planting crucifers because this will make the soil weaker. This is another reason why manure is not a suitable supplement to add to the cruciferous vegetable. It needs to be mixed into the soil, which calls for digging. Example vegetables are:

Broccoli	Kohlrabi
Brussels sprouts	Swedes (Rutabaga)
Cabbage	Turnips
Calabrese	Mustard cabbage
Cauliflower	Savoy cabbage
Kale	Collard greens

Komatsuna	Watercress
Choy Sum	Spinach
Siberian kale	Tatsoi
Radishes	Maca
Wasabi	Pak choi
Daikon	

Cucurbits

Cucurbits are a very diverse family of vegetables. From the size to the soil requirements, growth patterns (climbing, trailing, exactly where you plant them), and weather requirements, cucurbits do not subscribe to the one-size-fits-all standard. However, they all require a lot of nourishment to produce their large succulent fruits, so they need a similar method of garden preparation- a large amount of compost manure before sowing and then phosphate supplements later on to help the plants produce flowers and start blossoming to form your fruit. A great source of organic phosphorus is the tomato food plant or the comfrey. Both of these plants are rotted and diluted in water then watered directly at the plant base as a liquid feed.

Sowing any cucurbit vegetable is pretty easy. With a higher germination rate than pretty much any other seed-grown plant, you can be sure that many of the seeds you put into the ground will germinate. Which is why you should sow with care; cucurbits take up a lot of space and growing a lot of them together would choke them up. Some cucurbits like musk melons, some squashes, and cucumbers take well to vertical growth while others are simply too heavy to be suited for upwards growth.

Different cucurbits are ready for picking at different times in their growing season. Courgettes and cucumbers are

best harvested small. Their taste is better that way and the mother plant goes on to produce more when the older ones are picked. Pumpkin and squashes require to be thinned out, ensuring that all the nutrients go into a few fruits that grow to a huge size rather than having many small ones.

You will also need to protect your cucurbits from diseases like powdery mildew,   which can be done by removing infected leaves and spray a mixture of water and milk every week or so. Another thing to look out for is slug infestation. They directly affect the fruit and cause it to go soft. Cucumber mosaic virus is another common affliction of cucurbit vegetables. The only way to control this disease is to uproot the affected crop. And this affected plant should not be used as green manure or join the compost heap; destroy it permanently by, say, burning it. Below are some planting strategies for a few special cucurbits.

Pumpkins

Pumpkins come in a wide variety of sizes, from tiny colored pumpkins to giant Halloween types which are known to reach as much as 1,000 pounds. Pumpkins are spring vegetables so make sure that you sow them,   in a pot or into the ground, no later than mid-May. And because it is a trailing vegetable, space your pumpkins 30 inches apart in the row and along the column.

Pumpkins tend to rot when they are left to rest on wet ground. So be sure to place all your newly formed pumpkins on a plank to give them a better growing chance. You may also have to hand-pollinate the flowers for baby pumpkins to form. They will be ready to harvest before winter when their thick foliage dies away.

Marrows and Courgettes are planted in the same way as pumpkins. The only difference between pumpkins, marrows, and courgettes is that the former requires 40 inches of space because of their larger size.

Squash

There are two types of squash; summer and winter-growing squash. The squashes that grow in winter (harvested in the fall) are quite long lasting, but their summer counterparts are hard to store for any length of time. Their planting and care are   similar to that of pumpkins, except that they don't require as much space because they are relatively smaller.

Example vegetables are:

Squash	Cucumbers
Marrow	Gourds
Courgettes (Zucchini)	Watermelons
Pumpkins	Musk melons

Root vegetables

Root vegetables are an interesting lot in that the real vegetable grows out of sight. Any problems are only discovered upon harvesting, which is when you bring them to the surface to survey your handiwork. This, of course, means that problems with the crop cannot be mitigated during the growth period, unlike most other types that allow you to add supplements when your crop is not growing as well as you'd like. It is lucky that root vegetables also happen to be reasonably easy to grow. As long as your soil is right and you plant well, your root vegetables should give you a bumper harvest when the time comes to remove them from the ground, which should be in about three months for most roots crops.

Nitrogen is very important to the growth of root vegetables. If you can't rotate with leguminous crops to provide a natural endowment of nitrogen, consider manure, fertilizer, and compost. The sand should be light, with higher sand that clay in them, and deeply tilled to allow the roots to grow unhindered. Leeks and potatoes require a hilled topography (remove soil from the sides and pile on top of the column) but all other root crops are good to go on the flat surface of your garden. A top dress of nitrogen supplement a month after planting goes a long way in allowing your crop to develop bigger roots for a bumper harvest. Root vegetables are mostly grown in fall and spring seasons.   Their growth under the surface makes them cold-tolerant to a certain degree, but it is hard for the leaves to survive the heavy frost of winter.

Example vegetables are:

Beets	Artichoke
Carrots	Turnips
Kohlrabi	Black cumin
Potatoes	Sweet potato
Radishes	Parsley root
Konjac	Cassava
Chinese water chestnut	Ginger
Arrowhead	Bulrush
Cocoyam	Yams
Turmeric	Groundnuts
Ginseng	Tigernut

Alliums

Alliums are some of the most indispensable vegetables for humans around the world. They have also been around for millennia, featuring in Mongoloid diets, helping to sustain and strengthen Egyptian pyramid builders and the pillaging Roman armies. Alums are great at enhancing the taste of other foods and for that reason are a must-have for many recipes.

There are very many varieties of alum vegetables, but the onion features prominently as one that is grown and used by pretty much every civilization in the world. And even this single alum vegetable has numerous subtypes. Alliums are some of the easiest vegetables you could ever grow; they take very little space in the garden, require minimal attention, and you can grow them at any time of the year.

Alliums require finely ground soils. Any clumps should be broken up to ensure that your young plant encounters no resistance in sending out roots. Alliums are very resourceful vegetables in finding their own nutrients. They don't need a lot of supplements. In fact, too much of it and the flavor will be weak.

Example vegetables are:

Alliums	Spring onions
Onions	Scallions
Garlic	Shallots
Leeks	Chives

Different allium vegetables require different methods of planting. Onions, leeks, shallots, and chives are some common alliums that grow from seeds. Most others grow well from sets which are basically a small part of fully matured alliums that are taken apart and put into the ground to become a new plant. Sets are fast-maturing, (they have a huge head start on seeds), easier to handle, and require less maintenance once you have planted them. However, you will invariably have to pay more for sets than seeds.

When seeds are used, start them off in an indoor tray to give them a head start. This also ensures that the plant has a stress-free start-of-growth period, which should result in bigger bulbs later on.

Alliums are spring crops whether you grow them indoors first or plant directly in the garden. For the latter, April is the best time to put them into the ground while the former comes out of the tray and into the soil in mid-May.

Edible stem vegetables

Plant stem vegetables are very nutritional, but they are grown primarily as flavor-enhancing foods. From cinnamon to celery, asparagus, and rhubarb, edible stem vegetables are granted to make your meals  stand out for having a crunchy crispness to them, whether it is eaten as part of a salad or used in a recipe meal.

An indoors start to the growing season is desired for edible stem vegetables. Soak the seeds indoors for 10 and 12 weeks to ensure a better success rate once you take them out into the soil. These soils should be fertile and contain lots of organic matter, especially in the top layers because their roots are extremely shallow. Edible stem vegetables have a long season of growth (about 135 days) which has to be timed correctly to ensure that it falls smack in the middle of cool weather because they don't do well in the heat.

Once planted, a lot of water is needed to ensure that the plant grows to become fleshy and tender. Compost and mulch should be arranged around the plant for moisture retention and weeding should take place every week or so to ensure that the crop does not compete for nutrients at all. Just keep in mind the shallow roots when weeding so you don't damage your crop. Pull weeds out by hand- it's safer that way.

Example vegetables are:

Celery	Smilax
Asparagus	Bamboo shoots
Cardoon	Arctium
Celtuce	Humulus
Crithmum	Myoga
Heart of palm	Nopal
Rhubarb	Wild rice
Kohlrabi	

CHAPTER 7
SUPPLEMENTS FOR THE CROPS

Getting a bumper harvest out of your farm depends on the type of soil you have. A good soil will support healthy vegetables that can last you and your family a long time while a bad soil is likely to make a joke out of your hard work by producing less than you hoped. To create the perfect soil, you should add nutrients,   the mineral foods for plants and conditioners, and   the additives that bring out the best in your soil in terms of aeration, structure, acidity, and microorganisms. In this topic, we will look at all these materials at length.

Fertilizers

Fertilizers provide you with the most effective means of improving the nutritional properties of your soil in the short term. The effects of adding   fertilizer to your soil are   immediate and if lack of nutrients is the cause of your crops doing badly, the effects will be visible immediately. Plant nutrients exist in two main classes; micro and macro nutrients. Micro nutrients are not very influential to the health of the plant, but macro nutrients definitely affect plant growth. They include nitrogen, potassium, and phosphorous.

A deficiency of any macro nutrient will cause the crop to be weak and less productive. Nitrogen promotes green coloration and allows the plant to make their food. Deficiency of nitrogen is indicated by the yellowing of leaves and too much of it kills the plant. Phosphorous is responsible for the formation of fruits, flowers, and roots. Too little phosphorus   and your crops will experience stunted growth, with inferior flowers that produce even worse fruits. Finally, potassium accelerates plant growth. With no potassium, plants tend to experience stunted growth and yellowing leaves.

Macro nutrients may be introduced into the soil by two types of fertilizers; organic and inorganic. Inorganic fertilizers are mass-produced industrial products and even though they have higher nutrient content, they contain chemicals that ultimately end up in your dinner plate.

Organic fertilizers are made from the waste of naturally occurring animal and plant material like manure, cottonseed, and bone meal. Even though organic fertilizers contain a lower nutrient yield, their organic nature ensures a zero-impact situation as far as chemical pollution goes.

When buying fertilizer, we look at three numbers that are usually inscribed on the container to show the amount in pounds of macro nutrients contained in it. The nutrients are always listed starting with nitrogen, phosphorous, then potassium. A 100- pound bag of fertilizer inscribed with 10-20-10 indicates 10 pounds of nitrogen, 20 of phosphorous and 10 potassium for an overall yield of 40 pounds of nutrients. 60 pounds of the 100 pound of fertilizer is then filled with filler material like sand or rice hulls. They are usually materials that are beneficial to the soil, and in the case of rice hulls, they may actually add more benefits by adding organic matter.

The composition of fertilizers is usually a phosphorous content that is twice as much as the nitrogen and potassium. Some have no potassium at all because most soils contain enough of it already, but because potassium is a catalyst, it never harms to have more of it in your soil. You should absolutely steer clear of lawn fertilizers. They are often infused with weed control chemicals that harm your vegetables.

Other supplements that may be added with the fertilizer include lime;   adding calcium to soils with low pH to make them less acidic. To know what combination and quantity of fertilizer your soil needs, get it tested when you start out with your gardening journey, then retest every two years after that to keep up with the nutritional needs of your soil.

Applying fertilizers follows one of four ways ; broadcast, row application, starter solution, and side dressing. Broadcasting is done before planting by applying an even layer on top of the soil then mixing it up. It creates an even distribution of nutrients in the soil and makes it easier for crops to reach them. With row application, a small amount of fertilizer is added in the hole or ditch where the crop is to be planted. The one side effect of row distribution is that too much fertilizer coming in contact with plant roots may damage them.

Starter solutions are made by diluting a small amount of fertilizer (like 2 tablespoons) in about 1 gallon of water. A cup of the mixture is then poured in every hole meant for transplanting cabbage, tomatoes, pepper, or eggplants. Finally, side or top dressing is done by applying fertilizer to grown plants. The fertilizer used at the beginning of the planting season will most likely be fully consumed or drained away at this point, so adding more keeps the crops nourished.

They are great for immediate results, but you should be warned that fertilizers don't fix everything. Other deficiencies in your soil can only be fixed by the supplements discussed in this topic.

Worms

Apart from the nutritional properties of the soil, structure helps provide the right conditions for plant roots to do the crucial work of absorbing water, nutrients, and providing the plant with proper anchorage. Microbial organisms play a critical part in the formation of soils by eating at organic matter to make the soil richer.

The work of earthworms in the soil cannot be overstated. They are the biggest animals that live under the soil, so their work has a more distinct effect on the overall health of your soil. When earthworms eat at plant debris inside the soil, they release what turns out to be humus, a very important part of every soil. You'd be surprised to learn that worms are always eating. Or you might not be surprised at all;   there is no day or night under the surface after all, right? At any rate, scientists have unearthed very interesting facts about worms.

A recent study found that worms brought to the surface over 40 tons of soil in every hectare of cultivated land. Another study found that 90% of plant debris you leave on the ground is buried by worms. Clearly, worms are great allies in the fight to bring more fertility to your garden patch. The burrows left by earthworms are also very beneficial. They increase the seepage of water and air in your soil. While not all worms are good for your garden, most of them are and that is enough reason to think about how you can enhance their effectiveness on your soil.

Organic compost pit

Organic matter helps keep your soil healthy and conducive to plant growth. And while the nutritional yield of compost does not match the value of fertilizers, they also promote organic life and improve the structure of your soil. The compost pit is used to produce farmyard manure, combining things like rabbit, cow, and chicken droppings with household green waste, which is   anything from your garden that does not end up in your dinner table. You may also add any other waste material from the kitchen like banana peels, potato peels, and other common plant rubbish that can rot and disintegrate.

Compost can either be a hole dug into the ground (pit) or constructed at a workshop. To start a compost pit, dig a hole close to the garden and fill it with plant waste of all types. Over time, the rotting and fermenting creates a natural source of nourishment for your soil and ensures that your crops grow healthy and strong.

Any weeds taken out of the ground, the leaves, and organic waste from your kitchen can be thrown in the pit, but be careful, especially when adding weeds, so that your compost pit does not become a haven for weeds to hibernate awaiting introduction back into the soil. Other things that you can add to the compost pit include seaweed, a supplement that is high in nitrogen, potassium, and phosphorous and also effective in freeing up micro nutrients for when you plant. Straw and fall leaves make up for good compost and also come in handy in mulching your crops later on. Peanut shells improve air circulation in the soil and powdered rock introduces highly soluble micro and macro nutrients into the soil.

Until the plants have been broken down into organic matter, you should not use it in the garden. Turn your compost pit around with your fork or spade from time to time to take the top levels down below where the heat and the pressure of matter on top increases temperatures and allows them to break down faster. You should time the compost pit so that it is ready just before the next planting session then lay it out on top of the soil shortly before planting. 6 months is the ideal time to keep manure in your compost pit to allow for proper aging.

If you don't have some ground to dig into, substitute with a compost box. The compost pit or bin performs the most critical functions of farmyard manure development; it allows them to be broken down into nutritional components. Manure that has not been well matured before introduction to the garden tends to burn up your crops. This is caused by ammonia produced as a result of chemical reactions that break down organic matter.

Watering or irrigation

It almost goes without saying, but water is of paramount importance to the growth of any plant. Your vegetables need it more than anything else because a lot of their composition is water. Starting with the highest water content,   cucumbers and lettuce come first with 96% water in their total mass, followed by zucchini, radishes, and celery at 95%, tomatoes at 94%, and cabbages at 93%.

As such, they should have sufficient water in every stage of their life, from planting through to harvesting. To calculate the amount of water needed to keep your vegetables growing right, an inch of rainwater or 60 gallons in every 100 sq. ft should go into your vegetable patch every single week. If it rains, subtract the rainwater from the weekly ration and add the deficit. To know exactly how much water came down from natural precipitation, a rain gauge comes in handy for the serious gardener.

If you have ways of collecting rainwater, use it to water your vegetables. Tap water often contains chemicals from the treatment plant that may add minerals to your soil that may affect plant growth. That is as long as your area does not receive acidic rain, because that may be worse than tap water.

Another important thing to keep in mind is the depth your water   seeps into the soil. At the end of the day, plants don't absorb any water from the leaves. It all flows into the soil where the roots absorb it and transport it to the rest of the plant through the stem. Whether you use a hose pipe or a watering can, direct the water to the ground rather than the leaves. Directing the water also allows you to take charge of the areas where it lands. Anywhere other than close to the base of the plant leads to massive wastage and increases your workload in removing the extra weeds that you just helped get strong. If you can afford a drip irrigation system, install it in your garden and all your troubles will be sorted out. Drip irrigating your garden means that your workload in watering your plants is reduced and that the water is taken to the exact right place you need it to get to.

Watering should be done early in the day when the sun has not become too hot as to evaporate the water right out of your garden. The sun also dries up the water in your leaves and prevents the onset of fungal diseases that develop in overly watered leaves.

CHAPTER 8
PEST CONTROL

Insects can wreak havoc on your garden if left to run unchecked. Fortunately, many of the pest control methods that are available for gardeners tired of those jumping, crawling, or flying bugs are actually beneficial to the plants. And some of the most effective methods of pest control entail repurposing common gardening activities like planting, watering, mulching, weeding, pruning, and harvesting. In this topic, we discuss the common pests and how to eliminate them using organic methods and when that fails, going next level with pesticides.

Types of pests

Aphids

Aphids are small pear-shaped insects that favor the nutritional nourishment of plant sap of flowers, fruits, and vegetables. An aphid infestation will cause your plant to droop and distort. You may also spot a sooty mold growth

 on the surface of your vegetable leaves. The insects transport viral infections from one plant to another and if they have the flying range, from one garden to another. So look out for that beautiful growth of blossoming flowers that borders your vegetable garden. It may become a haven for pests that will trouble you with aphid infestations and viral disease transmission.

Cabbage maggot

Cabbage maggots are a pestilence of the cruciferous family of vegetables. These worms burrow under the surface and perforate holes at the base of your cabbage plant, cutting off the flow of water and nutrients to the plant and killing it. Where the maggot does not go all the way through and  instead digs a trench at the stem, it opens the cabbage up to disease-causing organisms.

Caterpillars

In the last chapter, we discussed worms as being beneficial to plant growth by helping to break down organic matter and aerating the soil. I also mentioned that some worms are destructive rather than beneficial. Well, the caterpillar is one of the more destructive worms. These multi-legged worms feed on leaves and dig into fruits, opening both to other disease-causing elements. A caterpillar infestation early in the life of a vegetable spells doom for the whole crop, especially if it is not controlled in time.

Cutworms

The cutworm is another worm that harms your vegetable garden. This huge, 1-inch nuisance with a segmented body targets the young shoots, burrowing through their tender stalks nightly at just above ground surface. If left unchecked, the cutworm can literally lay waste to your dream of starting a vegetable garden even before your crops leave the ground.

Tarnished plant bug

The tarnished plant bug is a spotted green-brown insect. This black-tipped wings and fast-moving bug feeds from the juices of your vegetables and causes the leaves to wilt and die from the tip downwards. It also feasts on young fruits of cucurbit vegetables and distorts them, stunting their growth and adversely reducing the yield from your garden.

Flea beetles

Flea beetles inhabit vegetable crops and chew through the leaves to leave tiny round perforations. They favor younger crops. In the meantime, their larvae could be hard at work feeding on the roots of your crops.

Colorado potato beetle

This pest targets the flowers of tomatoes, potatoes,

eggplants, and tomatoes, defoliating them and leading to lower yields down the line. They are identifiable from the black stripes on the wing covers of their yellow-orange bodies.

Mexican bean beetle

This beetle starts feasting on your garden patch from larvae stages, leaving your crops looking lacy and sickly. The larvae are dark yellow fat grubs and the adults have yellow-brown bodies and black spots on their wing covers.

• <u>Getting rid of pest</u>

While knowing how to identify the pests that seek to harm your crops is great, it would be very difficult to keep track of each and every one of them. Harder still would be trying to control each pest individually. Luckily, you can use a few pest control methods to control all the pests that may be present in your garden even without first having identified them all. First off, you should learn effective methods of preventing a pest infestation. If this does not work, there are a few effective methods of eliminating them.

Prevention

By now you must have heard the phrase "prevention is better than cure" a million and one times in different contexts. It is a cliché, but only because it works so well. In planning your garden, make an allowance for keeping it pest free so you don't have to rush when you start spotting the work of pests in dying plantings, defoliated blooms, or distorted fruits. If you can manage to prevent pests from coming into your garden in the first place, you will be saved a lot of grief and loss.

A lot of pests are transmitted through soils. If you have to buy soil from a different garden to use in yours, be conscious of the fact that pests lay their eggs inside the soil and these eggs hatch naturally to produce a new generation of root-burrowing, plant stem-eating, leaf-sucking vermin. However, the conditions created by natural fertilizers like compost manure and mulch are unfavorable for pest reproduction. For example, seaweed manure releases nutrients that actively repel slugs from the soil as well as improving the health of your crops and thus their ability to repel diseases and pest infestation. In essence, the healthier your soil is, the less likely you are to encounter a pest infestation. Creating a healthy soil therefore becomes the first step in keeping your garden pest free.

Just like animal predators, pests favor the weaker plants in your garden. If you spot a weak plant in your garden, it will either be infected or be a target for future infestation. Pull it out and throw it away, preferably far from your garden. If you want to be more clinical in your pest elimination, examine these weaker plants and try to see what caused its weakness. You might be surprised the kind of information you will gather from that simple task. It could be the key to saving the rest of your garden if you identify the cause before it spreads to other plants.

Crop rotation and inter-planting are great ways to kill off pests by reducing their rate of reproduction. Most pests are specific to some types of crops and will die off if they can't feed on the leaves, stems, or roots of a certain crop. If you skip planting their preferred crop through crop rotation, they will inevitably starve to death. Inter-planting prevents pests from spreading all over your garden by the same concept of plant-specific pest infestation. If a pest can't just move one crop over and feed on its preferred crop, then other plants of the same type are free from infestation.

Elimination

However much you try to prevent pests from invading the sanctity of your garden, it is almost inevitable that they will attack your crops. In elimination, the key thing is to ensure that you don't harm your soil or the rest of your crops as you attempt to get rid of pests. Synthetic insecticides leaching into a runway can   end up   in water sources and ultimately find   their way into the atmosphere; they are responsible for much of the pollution that is caused by farming activities. Organic pest elimination is the way to go as it has a less negative impact on the environment. Even better, you can make these pest-control remedies at home using common household supplies and they'll work just as fine.

For soft bodied   insects like aphids and mites, a single tablespoon or vegetable oil (like canola) mixed with a millimeter of ivory soap works wonders when mixed with water and sprayed all over the plant. Be sure to direct the spray at the underside of leaves to reach all pests. The oil in this simple concoction smothers all insects and their larvae on the plant.

Mites can be eliminated by spraying with a solution of 1 millimeter of ivory soap with 2 tablespoons of cayenne pepper (hot pepper works just as well). The solution should then be left in a bottle for one night to mature properly then stirred before applying.

For grubs like the larvae of beetle pests, a very effective and long lasting remedy is the milky spore. While milky spore is store-bought and is not a homemade remedy, it is completely organic and is extremely effective as a one-off solution. Dead grubs only increase the effectiveness of spores in the soil that kill off new grubs and since they don't grow to maturity as beetles, your garden will soon be totally rid of beetles and grubs within a few years of the first application. Milky spore has the distinction of being one of the few organic solutions to pest infestation that does not harm other pests.

Fungal diseases are easily eliminated by mixing 2 tablespoons of baking soda in every gallon of water used in spraying your crops. Keep adding baking soda to your water till your crops are disease-free. As for powdery mildew, Neem oil added to spraying water or milk and mixed   in a 1:1 ratio does the trick.

The painful truth of pest elimination, even organic non-toxic ones made at home, is that they don't discriminate harmful insects from beneficial ones. To ensure that your garden remains with beneficial insects, you should combine prevention with elimination. If you intercrop your garden and a certain crop gets infested, your spraying it with pesticide will remove all insects in that particular plant, but the beneficial ones will still be surviving on the other crop and can always move back in, this time without sharing the plant with destructive pests.

CHAPTER 9

WHAT CAN I PLANT IN DIFFERENT SEASON?

100 list of crops to plant in 4 seasons

- *20 Vegetables You Can Plant In Winter*

While some may not know this, food crops are naturally hardy and as such cope just fine in cold winter months. These crops are not only hardy; you can plant most of them outdoors as well. This way, even in winter, your garden is in use and fully stocked.

If you would like to know how to grow vegetables in winter but unsure which and how to plant, we have provided the answers you need in this section on **vegetables you can plant in winter**. Read on

Plant	Soil	Planting Instructions	Harvest time
Beets	Fertile loam soil	Planted by the seeds, this cold tolerant plant should be planted deep inside the soil. They thrive best on loose soil with a pH around 6.5-7.0. Work in some aged compost into the soil. In high pH soil, add some quantity of kelp meal or a boron-rich fertilizer. Boron besides other soil nutrients is especially important for beet. A deficiency of boron in the soil could lead to stunted and bushy	At about 1inch in diameter, you can start harvesting baby beets. At 2 inches most varieties of beet should be ready for harvest. Harvest by pulling the root of as many as you want and leave the rest to mature further. However, do not allow them grow over stay in the soil as they turn woody and

| | | tops with cankers in the root.

Ensure you follow the package instructions as very little boron goes a long way. | tough with time. |
|---|---|---|---|
| **Carrots** | Loam soil/regular garden soil | Just like beet, carrot is low-maintenance and thrives even in the cold winter months.

There are different types of carrots but they're categorized into the following five groups:

Chantenay, Denver, Nantes, Specialty and **Imperator.**

To plant, dig soil to break up all clumps of soil. Also remove rocks before planting.

Use only aged manure (up to 2 | While it's possible to pull carrots by their tops during harvest, the baby carrots which are usually ready within 50-60 days may not be strong enough to pull by the leaves.

To effectively harvest the carrots, loosen the soil with a garden fork and pick the carrots. |

		years) or the high nitrogen content in many fertilizers may cause your harvest to become forked and hairy.	Carrots should be matured enough for harvest in 75 days.
		For extra delicious carrot, sprinkle a small amount of wood ash on the planting bed and rake into the first few inches of soil.	
		The potassium from wood ash helps to boost the soil pH if low.	
		Drill between 4-5cm deep and plant the seeds. Cover with earth once planted.	
		Compared to many winter plants, carrots may take some time to germinate. If everything goes well, seedlings	

| | | should emerge within 1 to 2 weeks.

The slow ones could take longer but an extra week should be enough.

Carrots do better in moist soils so make sure your new beds are sufficiently-hydrated. | |
|---|---|---|---|
| **Leeks** | Loamy/re gular garden soil | Possibly one of the hardiest vegetables, leeks are easy to grow and almost pest free.

There are two types of leeks and they are:

Summer leeks and **winter leeks**.To plant leek, make holes between 10-15cm deep with a stick and at 25-30cm spacing.

Water leeks well and then place as | Once the plants reach your desired size, they can be harvested.

Simply loosen the soil around the quantity you need with a garden fork and pull out. |

		single plants in the open holes. You can cover the bed with insect-proof mesh to protect them from leek moth and other pests. For nutrient, add compost manure or granular organic fertilizer as they grow.	
Peas		One of the vegetables that thrive well in colder temperatures, peas comes in several varieties: **Sugar Snap, Sugar Daddy, Sugar Mel etc.** They are mostly grown for their inner pods and are eaten raw or cooked. Planting is easy. Work 2-3 inches of manure to the soil.	Usually, peas are ready between 65 to 70 days. However one of the best ways to tell at this period is by tasting them. Harvest can last between two to three weeks.

		You can choose to soak the dry seeds overnight in water before planting or plant directly. Plant the seeds 1 inch deep in double rows, spacing the seeds. Leave about 4 to 6 inches spaces between the plants. Allow up to 2 feet between each of the rows for ease of access.	
Asparagus		Asparagus does well in the cold winter months without any special attention. Like most vegetable crops, it requires the essentials like nutrients and moisture to thrive. Soak the seeds between 24-48hrs before planting.	Create an area within the greenhouse or garden for yearly growth or map out a section within your green house or in a pot. And enjoy once mature.

		They could take between 2-8 weeks to germinate and expect about 75% to germinate under favorable conditions.	
Radishes	Well-drained garden soil	Radishes come in **icicle, cherry bell** and **champion** varieties. They grow pretty fast too and within 6 weeks they should be ready for harvest. While they're great for inter-planting, they do well on their own. Plant the seeds between ¼ and ½ inches deep. Radishes do not need large amounts of manure or composts. Too much of it would boost the	In about 30 days, the radishes should be ready for harvest. Dig the floor around it with a garden fork then pull out as many as you need.

		foliage but do little for the roots.	
Collards	Loamy soil	A non-heading member of the cabbage family, they do great in the winter. They come in the **Georgia, Vates,** and **Blue Max** varieties. They are excellent for direct seeding in the garden. Typically, they do better in a soil pH between 6.0 - 6.5. Plant the seeds 5 inches apart and allow 25 inches between the rows. Be wary of cabbage pests like cabbage worms or fluttering moths.	Collards are ready for harvest within 65-75 days. Harvest season can last 4 to 30 depending on the quantity grown and needed.
Pak Choi/	Rich moisture-	Work some amounts of aged manure or compost	Typically, baby greens are ready to be

Chinese Mustard Cabbage	retentive loamy soil	into the already prepared soil. Sprinkle the seeds 2 – 4 inches apart. And in super-frosty weather, cover with a lightweight row cover. Also cover if cabbage pests become a problem.	harvested in 30 days. The mature plant can be harvested at once by cutting at soil level or picking the baby leaves when needed.
Kale	Soil rich in organic matter	The highly nutritious kale is a year round vegetable. This means it grows even in the cold winter months. There are three types of kale and they are: **Scotch kale, Siberian kale, and 'Lacinato kale'**. In winter, you can grow kale by planting in the cold frame and transplanting the	Pick the leaves as you need them. Kale should however be ready for harvest within 55-65 days.

		young seedlings to the garden. For direct seeding, plants seeds 2-3 inches apart, thinning later to 12 inches once true leaves begin to appear. Leave up to 2 feet between each row.	
Turnips	Boron-rich garden soil with even moisture	Another easy vegetable to grow, turnips are not demanding at all. They are grown for both their greens and roots. Sow the seeds in a garden bed spacing 7 – 8 inches. Also, they can be grown in containers or pots for their roots or the tops.	The greens of turnips are usually ready for harvest within 30 days and the roots within 60 days. Cut off the top leaving about 2 inches of foliage. Roots can be harvested at baby stage or at about to 2-3

			inches in diameter.
Swiss Chard	Nutrient-rich loamy soil	A member of the beet family, the Swiss chard is a hardy vegetable that thrives even in frosty months. Plant the seeds 2 inches apart in a soil pH between 6.0 – 7.0 Space the row a foot apart and cover the bed with a row cover. This helps to protect it from unexpected temperature drops and freezes. You can plant fresh seeds each week for successive crops.	Swiss chard can be harvested by picking the outer leaves while leaving the center to grow more and also by cutting the adult plant to a stub around 2-3 inches. The baby leaves should be ready for harvest in 5 – 6 weeks while the adults may need extra four or six weeks to mature enough for harvest.
Lettuce	Nutrient-rich loamy soil	Simply sprinkle lettuce seeds in specific areas of the garden or between	The leaves are ready for harvest once

		slower-growing plants. Mix slightly for good contact with the soil. Water and mark with a plant tag if you want. Keep your eyes open for slugs or aphids as they are fairly common with lettuce.	they mature and turn a light shade of green
Onions	Nutrient-rich loamy soil	Onions are hardy plants that can survive the cold winter months even outside greenhouses. Plant the seeds 2 inches deep, 14 – 36 inches between the row and 2-3 inches between the plants.	The onions are set for picking between 3-4 weeks after planting. And they're easy to harvest; simply give them a gentle pull and shake off any clinging soil.

		Onions require a steady supply of water but don't overdo it and remember to cut down on watering some weeks before harvest as they are best dried before harvest for good storage quality.	
Irish potatoes	Well-drained nutrient-rich soil	A year round vegetable, potatoes grow well in frosty winter months. They should be sprouted before planting. They can also be planted whole if tiny or split into 2 inch pieces.	You'll know it's time for harvest when the star-shaped flowers begin to appear. For a baby crop, you can dig out some at this point and let the rest continue to mature.

| | | Allow the split pieces sit in a cool dry place for a day or two so the fresh cuts heal enough before they hit the soil as they may rot if not done.

A soil pH within 5.0 to 6.5 is ideal to prevent scab, a common potato disease. | This is usually between 70 – 120 days. |
|---|---|---|---|
| **Mustard green** | Rich, moist soil | While not as hardy as kale and collards, mustard greens do well in winter.

They can tolerate a light frost and if it becomes unbearable cold, put some shredded leaves or straws around the plant. | To harvest, you can start by picking the outside leaves of the baby plant.

Unless you need everything, you should leave the rest to mature as you pick the ones |

		Not-so-hardy crops like the mustard green should be planted in a simple cold frame. For additional insulation add some straw or shredded leaves around the crop. Plant the seeds ¼ inch deep and space 2 inches between the plants and 12 inches spacing in rows.	you need when you want. On average, both baby and mature mustards are ready for harvesting between 21 – 45 days
Arugula	Fertile garden soil	A cold-hardy green that thrives in any weather, the Arugula is unbelievably easy to plant.	In 30 days or less, the spicy green is set for harvesting.

		Simply sprinkle the seeds on already prepared soil and scratch it in a bit with a rake. You can add a layer of floating row cover inside structure for additional insulation.	Start by cutting the outer leaves once they are at least 2 or 3 inches long and leave the rest to continue producing fresh harvests.
Mizuna	Nutrient rich soil.	This slightly bitter foliage is categorized under the Asian family of mustards. Mizuna can be planted as a seed directly in the garden or started indoors and the seedlings moved into the garden. In cold winter, mizuna can be used to fill in empty	Baby plants can be picked in about 20 days while full heads are ready in 50 days. To harvest, clip the baby leaves or cut at the head when mature.

| | | areas in cold frames.

Sprinkle the seeds on the already prepared soil. | |
|---|---|---|---|
| **Tatsoi** | Nutrient-rich well-drained soil | This attractive plant is not only cold-hardy but also a delicious addition to winter salads and stir-fries.

The seeds can be planted directly in gardens or indoors under light.

Plant the seed on prepared soil about ½ deep and allow about 1 inch space between.

To harvest all winter, plant in several batches and | To harvest baby leaves, cut the leaves once they are four inches long.

Mature tatsoi can be cut at the stem. |

		grow in a cold frame.	
Cabbage	Nitrogen-rich well-amended soil	Available in several varieties including the **Round Green types, Red Rookie** and **Stonehead,** Plant indoors for about 12 weeks, and then move the garden. Cover with beds with row cover or cloches to protect from frost. When planting, allow up to 16 to 18 inches of space between. Compact cabbage types may be planted together	Cabbages are ready for harvest when the heads are full and firm. Cut at the base of the head if you'll need it right away. If you'll be storing away, pull up the whole plant including the root and wrap in a newspaper. Place in a cool, humid area like the basement.

		while larger ones require more space	If stored properly, the plants should keep for many months.
		Cabbages need a steady supply of water to thrive so, to help retain moisture, place shredded leaves on top of the soil.	
Parsley	Nutrient-rich soil	Cold-hardy biennial, parsley can grow all year.	As the plant grows, cut off outer stalks continuously for use unless of course you need them all at once.
		However, you have to protect it from snow and hard frosts else it dies.	
		To plant, first soak the seeds for up to 24hrs to increase its chances of germinating.	This way, you're assured of a steady supply of fresh leaves.
		Plant the seeds in a cold frame protected from the icy winter weather.	

		Space the seeds 12 inches apart and the rows 18 to 20 inches apart.	
Broccoli	Nutrient-rich garden soil	Broccoli tolerates winter and will thrive in several severe frosts. It should be started indoors about 75-95 days before your first frost date. Transplant to your garden at three weeks old. Also, it has to be supplied regularly with water to grow well.	Your broccoli is ready for harvest when the heads begin to near their maximum size and the bud still closed (according to your specific seed pack). Alongside 3 to 5 inches of stem, cut the center head allowing the side shoots to mature and extend the harvest for some extra weeks.

		Broccoli thrives on soil pH between 6.0- 6.8	
		Look out for caterpillars and cabbage worms and toss out any you find.	
		Cover with a row cover if need be to keep out any pests.	

20 Vegetables You Can Plant In Spring

After winter, comes spring. It is time to plant again in the sun. Now, while the abovementioned crops are classified under crops you can plant in winter, they perform excellently in spring. This time however, there are little restrictions as the weather is perfect for almost everything.

So, in the table below, we've outlined a number of nutritious vegetables you can plant in spring

Plant	Soil	Planting Instructions	Harvest time
Peppers	Nutrient rich soil with moisture	Almost every pepper is a warm season vegetable. They come in several varieties with the popular ones being **habaneros, cayenne,** and **bell pepper** amongst so many others. Generally, peppers are categorized into two main types; hot peppers and sweet peppers. Start the peppers 8-11 weeks before your last frost.	Most peppers are ready for harvest once they reach the preferred size. Some types are however picked when they are 3 to 4 inches long. For the colored ones, ripening is sign of maturity and they can be harvested then.

		Place the plants at the hottest points in the garden, if possible the areas where the snow melts first. Transplant in a grid style on 16-inch centers or space each plant 18 inches apart. Keep the plants sufficiently supplied with water. Also, watch out for aphids as they like to bunch on the top of the plant.	Cut instead of pulling to avoid destroying the plants or harvest.
Sweet potatoes	Moist nutrient-dense soil	Sold as slips by most seed companies, (slips are green shoots just beginning to form roots), they are commonly	Sweet potatoes are ready for harvest with 90 – 120 days

		available for sale in April.	after transplant.
			To harvest, loosen the soil around each plant.
		Now, at this point, may not be warm enough for them to go outside as sweet potatoes need heat to survive.	You do not want to destroy the crop, so watch where the prongs go.
		You can start your own slip.	
		Simply purchase some organic potatoes from a supermarket.	
		Set them on moist soil or partly submerged in water, and store in a cool place.	
		It could take a few months for slips to form.	

		Once they are formed, remove them carefully and plant halfway in the already prepared soil. Watch out for potato beetle and other pests and remove with your hands or rinse out once you see them. You can protect the plant with a row cover or insect barrier	
Eggplant	Nutrient-rich loamy soil	Heat-loving and cold-sensitive veggies, eggplants are the perfect spring vegetables. They come in many varieties. Before planting, start the seeds indoors some 7-8	Try pressing the skin mildly with your finger. It is ready to be harvested if the flesh gives and

		weeks before your last frost.	bounces back.
		Transfer the seedlings to your already prepared soil. Space them on 20 inch centers.

They thrive on water so supply regularly with water. | But if too hard to allow an indentation, then it's probably too young to be harvested. |
| | | Do not fertilize with nitrogen-rich fertilizers during the growing season as it may result in healthy leaves and small fruits. | Remove fruit regularly so production stays high. |
| **Tomatoes** | Nutrient-dense soil with moisture | One of the best spring plants, tomatoes remain some of the most popular garden | Depending on the tomatoes, the color and size should be enough to |

		vegetables everywhere.	determine maturity.
			You can pick at that point.
		There are several types and planting them is easy.	
		However, they require a long planting season and as such need to be grown first indoors under lights for about 7 – 10 weeks.	
		Prepare the garden and work a considerable amount of manure into the soil to boost the nutrient levels then transplant.	
		While tomatoes are easy to plant, they	

| | | require some tender care and a steady supply of water.

For moisture and to prevent the spread of diseases and weeds, a thick mulch layer should do. This can either be shredded leaves or straw. | |
|---|---|---|---|
| **Rhubarb** | Nutrient-dense well-drained soil | One of the first sweet vegetables of spring, rhubarb is a perennial vegetable.

Planting rhubarb is super-easy. Prepare the garden and ensure the area is well-drained and fertile.

Your one year rhubarb should be planted in early | Rhubarbs are ready for harvest once they are 12-18 inches long.

Harvest by pulling the plant with a light twist. You can also choose to cut the stalk at the base. |

		spring once the ground becomes workable. Spacing about 4 feet apart, plant the roots 2-3 inches below the soil's surface. The plants need all the manure they can get so ensure they're fed ample amounts of it. Avoid adding chemical fertilizers with nitrates as they can kill the plants at first contact.	
Corn	Fertile well-drained soil	An annual crop with many different colors, corn loves spring! It is wind-pollinated and as such has to be	Harvesting can begin 2 – 3 weeks after the silk appear. To confirm, pick one

		planted in blocs instead of single rows.	and pull back some part of the husk.
		Start planting the grains two weeks after the last frost date.	The grains should be plump and smooth when mature. The liquid should also be milky when pinched with a fingernail and the silk turning brown.
		This is important because corn like most grains would need a relatively lengthy period in warm weather to thrive.	
		Plant the seeds 1 inch deep and 8 inches apart.	
		Rows should 25 – 30 inches apart.	
		Water adequately and cover with a	

		with a floating row cover to trap heat and protect from pests like birds. Lift the covers every two days to supply with moisture until they germinate. Lastly, they're susceptible to common garden pests such as raccoons, cutworms, cucumber beetle etc. so watch out for those.	
Pumpkins	Well-drained nutrient-rich soil	A long-growing spring plant, pumpkins are easy to maintain once there is no danger of frost.	Only harvest pumpkins when they are large and mature enough. the

		Because the vine varieties need a lot of space to crawl, you'll need to pick a site with plenty of space.	color change into a deeper solid color is one of the first signs. Another way to find out is by pressing your thumb against the pumpkin. It is ripe if it resists puncture.
		Plant the seed 1 inch deep into specially created "pumpkin mounds".	
		With the right temperature and soil, the seeds should germinate in a week or less and spring up in 5 to 10 days.	
		At 2 – 3 inches tall, thin down to 2 – 3 plants per hill and rows space 7 – 10 feet apart.	

		Cover with row covers early in the season to protect from pests but remember to remove covers right before it flowers to enable insects pollinate. Pumpkins needs to be supplied with water and weeds kept out.	
Cucumber	Nutrient-rich soil	The typical warm season vegetable, cucumbers come in various sizes and shapes. Planting is easy. Prepare the soil and supply with aged manure. They are climbing plants and as such best planted next to	Within 50 – 80 days from planting, the cucumbers should be mature enough for harvest. You can start

		fences or crops like corn.	picking then. Ensure however that you pick often to prevent the fruits from over maturing.
		These also serve as windbreaks, and moisture is also trapped for the cucumber in the process.	
		In direct seeding, plant 1 inch deep and 2 inches apart. When sprouted, thin to about 7 – 10 inches.	
		Leave about 5 feet between each row if unsupported. If you live in a region with long growing seasons, you can plant new seeds fortnightly until midsummer.	
		But make certain the variety you	

		pick will have enough time to mature before winter comes.	
		Watch out for common pests like aphid, cucumber beetles and squash borers.	
		Protect newly planted crops from infestation by covering with a row cover or insect barrier	
		Also, supply cucumbers with adequate water as too little may cause you to have a bitter yield	

| Snap Beans | Fertile, well-drained soil | Unlike pole beans, bush beans aka snap beans mature really quickly.

They can be directly seeded in the garden and because they are warm season crops, they do very well in sunny spots.

Avoid planting under a shade or in waterlogged soil as they will likely rot. A pH around 6.0 – 7.0 is best.

Plant snap beans seed an inch deep when the frosty period ends and the soil warms up.

You can hasten the warming by | As they grow quickly, ensure you pick once they start to produce.

Once passed maturity, they should be removed. Pick only snap beans with small, smooth and crisp pods for the best taste. |

		covering the patch with black plastic a week or two before you plant. This aids germination and protects the newly planted seeds from birds and other pests.	
Spinach	Nutrient-dense soil	Used in salads and cooking, spinach is a truly versatile plant. The succulent and smooth leaves grow well in spring. Plant by sowing into rows about 12 – 15 inches apart.	Harvest should be ready in 30 days. Cut little and frequently as you do not want the leaves to grow too big. If you decide to plant more, cover with

		Thin the seeds 8 inches apart. While spinach needs sunlight to grow, things can go awry quickly in hot weather. To prevent this, sow in lightly shaded areas during hot months. Also, supply with water regularly to keep the ground moist.	a row cover to protect from the weather as it gets cooler.
Garlic	Decent, well-drained soil	Completely low-maintenance, its flavor is on a league of its own and as such deserves a mention.	You'll know your crop is mature enough for harvest when half

the leaves turn brown.

Ordinarily, garlic is an excellent fall plant but in spring however, you can still enjoy its green shoots if you want.

It comes in two main varieties and they are; **hardneck** garlic and **softneck** garlic.

To harvest, loosen the soil around the plant with a garden fork.

To plant, find a sunny area within the garden with well-drained fertile soil.

Make furrows with the handle of your hole and space one foot apart. Make a shallow hole about 3 inches deep.

Pull the mature stalk gently to free it from the soil.

Handle carefully as damage can affect storage.

		Plant each of the preselected garlic bulbs between 3 – 4 inches deep and space about 6 – 8 inches apart in the rows.	
Cilantro	Nutrient dense well-drained soil	One of the best herbs to grow in spring, it is easy to plant cilantro from the seed.	It blooms once it reaches maturity.
		It enjoys sunlight so plant in the area your garden enjoys the most light.	You either harvest the seeds and use in your meals or leave some on the stem to be blown off for reseeding at the next planting season.
		Plant 2 inches deep and space out 12 inches between the rows.	

Kohlrabi	Rich, well-drained soil	A cool weather crop, Kohlrabi thrives in early spring. It can be planted in a cold frame or directly in the garden.	Start picking kohlrabi once the stems are up to 2 – 3 inches in diameter.
		The seeds can be started indoors for up four weeks before transplanting to the garden.	To pick, cut the stem two inches beneath the bulb. You can also trim off leaves for use in steamed greens or salads.
		Before planting, prepare the soil with one or two inches of compost. This should be in a sunny space.	
		Plant the seeds about ½ inch deep and 2 inches apart.	

		Later thin to 4 inches with some of the thinning carefully moved to other places in the garden to optimize production. Space the rows about a foot apart For a long harvest, sow fresh seeds every 21 days from mid-spring to late spring.	
Cauliflower	Nutrient-rich well amended soil with aged manure	Cauliflower is a great vegetable for spring. It requires a not-too-hot or too cold weather to thrive. Though considered as one of the most	Cauliflowers are ready for harvest once the heads are big enough, aim for 6 to 8 inches across. Cut the head off and pull out

		difficult crops to grow, with the care and soil, cauliflower will do just fine.	the entire plant for use in the compost pile.
		To plant, work in the organic manure with soil pH between 6.0 and 7.0	
		While it can be grown directly with the seeds, it is better started indoors for about 5 weeks and transplanted into the garden.	
		Space out the plants on 18 inch center.	
		Extra early spring cauliflowers may	

		need to be covered with a row cloth for insulation. Frequently vent and remove when the weather stabilizes.	
Bountiful basil	Fertile garden soil	There are several varieties of basil available and you can opt for any. The plant grows well when planted directly. But you can also grow indoors until the seedlings appear and transfer to decently fertile soil. Once they are about 2 inches tall, separate and	Basil should be ready for harvest within 70 – 80 days after planting. Harvest the leaves by cutting back about the third of the plant's height. Ensure you only cut above the leaves instead of

		replant 7 inches apart.	leaving stubs.
			The plant should be ready for harvest again a few weeks.
Brussels sprouts	Fertile soil with even moisture	When cooked right, Brussels sprouts are as tasty as can be.	Plants are ready for harvest within 80 to 100 days.
		An excellent spring vegetable, they enjoy sunny spots in the sun in a nutrient-dense soil.	Pick the biggest sprouts on the stems bottom as you work your way to the top.
		Before planting work a considerable amount of organic manure into the soil.	

They can be directly planted but best if they are started indoors for about 4 weeks before moving to the garden.

Space out the seedlings on 18 inch centers and 24 inches apart in each row.

They belong in the cabbage family and as such are susceptible to cabbage pests such as cabbage worms and cabbage loopers.

To prevent damages from these pests cover the bed with a row

		cover immediately you plant. Pick or rinse out foliage-eating slugs.	
Raspberries	Well-drained fertile soil	Raspberries remain some of the easiest plants to grow even with minimal care. There are two basic classifications of raspberry; the **summer-fruiting raspberries** and **the Ever-bearing** bearing ones. You can plant any. Pick a site with full sun and a well-drained area.	All varieties of raspberries should begin to yield fruits in their second season though Ever-bearers may yield some small berries in their first autumn. Pick berries every few days when they ripen.

		Prepare soil with compost weeks before planting.	
		Soak roots for an hour or two and plant in holes wide enough for spreading.	
		Keep the crown 1 or 2 inches above the ground and space each plant 2 – 3 feet apart and 8 feet apart in rows.	
		You can support with a trellis a fence depending on the variety you plant.	

| Okra (lady's finger) | Fertile well-drained soil | Not only is the okra plant beautiful and rich in nutrients, planting it is easy.

You can start planting indoors 5 weeks before the last frost date or plant the seeds directly in spring.

Soak in water overnight to accelerate germination.

Plant 1 inch deep and 15 to 18 inch apart.

For transplants, space 1 to 2 feet to give them sufficient space to grow. | On average, the okra plant will be ready for harvesting 2 months after planting.

Harvest when around 2 to 3 inches long. Remember to wear gloves when harvesting okra as most varieties of the plants are covered with tiny spines that can prick your skin. |

		Watch out for common okra pests like aphids, corn earworms and stinkbugs.	
Zucchini/squash	Moist, well-drained soil	Divided into two categories, squash are amazing producers. So great are they at producing that at their peak season, they'll produce so many squashes in a day. To plant, first work plenty of compost into the already prepared soil. Plant seeds about an inch deep and up to 3 feet apart. Water once in a week but not shallowly. Moisture needs to	Most varieties of squash are matured in 60 days. Cut off the fruit from the vine instead of breaking them up. You can store freshly harvested squash in your refrigerator for up to ten days.

		go about 4 inches down.	
		Watch out for pests like the squash vine borer, aphids, sting bug, squash bug, and cucumber beetle.	
Rutabagas	Rich, well-drained soil	Plant rutabaga seeds ½ deep directly in the garden. Space out the rows 12 to 18 inches. Flea and beetles are common rutabaga pests so you want to cover immediately with a row cover after planting. Thin 6 inches apart once seedlings are	For best tasting crop, harvest only when the roots are about 4 to 5 inches across. If you want, you can leave the rutabagas in the ground exposed to the cool air before

		about 4 inches tall. Water weekly	harvesting and storing.

• *20 Plants You Can Plant In Summer*

Even as the cool season draws to an end and the warm season approaches, it is not too late at all to plant vegetables in the garden.

True, some plants are better suited for the cooler times of the year, but when handled well, most will perform amazingly in summer.

There are also varieties of summer plants naturally suited for the hot summer months and by fall; most should be ready for harvest.

In this section, we've outlined a number of vegetables that you can plant in the summer and obtain amazing results.

Plant	**Soil**	**Planting Instructions**	**Harvest time**
Leaf amaranth	Nutrient-rich garden soil	Although less common than many garden vegetables, the leaf amaranth is certainly worth	The Leaf amaranths are ready for harvest once they grow

		giving a try in your summer garden.	about two to four inches tall.
			You should be able to get up to 3 harvests before you need to plant a different batch.
		The sweet and slightly tangy-tasting vegetables work in many dishes from stir-fries to salads.	
		It is heat-tolerant and that makes it a good candidate to compete for space in your summer garden unlike spinach or kale.	
		Planting is easy; scatter the tiny seeds on prepared and nutrient-rich soil.	
		Watch out for leaf miners, although rare with the plant,	

		they can become a problem.	
Red bell pepper	Nutrient-dense soil	A plant rich in vitamins A, B6, and C, planting red bell pepper is incredibly easy plus it thrives in the hot months. To grow in containers in the warm summer months, plant one pepper in a pot with a depth of about 8 – 12 inches. A nutrient-dense soil with moisture is essential for growing healthy plants. The two commonest pests of the red bell	Red bell peppers are mature enough for harvest once they turn red. Pick as needed

		peppers are aphids and fleas. Watch out for them and control their effects with organic homemade sprays like the tomato leaf spray or the hot pepper spray. They are both effective.	
Cherry tomatoes	Decently fertile loamy soil	Cherry tomatoes are probably one of the easiest tomatoes to grow. Unlike regular tomatoes that may be tricky for beginners, cultivating cherry tomatoes is almost a breeze.	They are mature enough for harvest once their colors change to deep red hue.

		Simply find a sunny area for the tomato in a decently fertile ground. Ensure the soil for their root is deep enough. Plant them in the same depth and row spaces like you would regular tomatoes. As they grow tall, support with trellises or sticks.	
Rainbow chard	Decently fertile soil	Rainbow chards are beautiful additions to any summer garden.	The rainbow chards are ready for harvest once they attain a height of about six to nine inches.

		The highly nutritious plant can grow up to two feet tall with its bright red stems. It is also one plant that thrives in summer as much as it does in spring. Plant the seeds ½ inches and space 2 inches apart in an already prepared decently fertile soil	
Edible flowers (nasturtium)	Decently fertile garden soil	Edible flowers like nasturtium are easy additions to all summer gardens. They come in several varieties with the same trademark taste of	It should be ready for harvest in two to four weeks. Snip off the flower and petal with scissors and it is ready to be eaten.

		the floral variety of arugula.	
		While it is a great summer plant, nasturtium would need a little shade when it gets too hot.	
		Plant the seeds in ½ to ¼ inches of soil. You can choose to grow indoors in pots.	
Bok Choy	Nutrient-rich garden soil	Bok Choy is a vegetable rich in vitamin A and many antioxidants. Depending on the type you plant, Bok Choy can add beauty to your	The plant is ready for harvest once it is about 3 – 4 inches tall. You can either harvest by cutting the quantity you need or the entire head if it's a one-time harvest.

		meal besides the nutrients it parks. To thrive, Bok Choy needs the warm summer sun though can use some shade during very hot days. Plant 8 to 12 inches apart and 1 inch deep in nutrient-rich garden soil.	
Tomatillos	Well-drained decently rich soil	Closely related to tomatoes, eggplants and pepper, tomatillo's green fruits are perfect for many cooking needs.	Tomatillos will be ready for harvest within 75 to 100 days after the transplant.

		To grow, select a well-drained decently rich portion of your garden as they do not do well in poorly drained ones.	
		Work some amounts of compost into the soil.	
		Plant the already started tomatillo seeds like you would a tomato.	
		Space the rows 4 feet apart and the plants 3 feet apart to give them the space to spread.	
		You can also provide gardening trellises or tomato	

		cages to keep them above the ground.	
Muskmelon	Fertile soil with plenty of compost	Delicious muskmelons perform well in summer. Plant by sowing seeds 1 inch deep and space out when you thin. To prevent damages by insect and aid the growth, cover the seedlings after planting with row cover until they bloom. Small melons mature quickly on average and also take up less space than the big ones.	Muskmelons begin to separate naturally from their stems when ripe. This makes harvesting easy as a gentle pull is all that is needed.

Malabar spinach	Decently fertile well-drained soil	This fast growing plant is packed with nutrients and will overtake most other garden plants in no time. Sow seeds in late spring when the soil becomes warm enough to plant. Move to the garden and support with a trellis as it grows.	Harvest as much as you need for your meals.
Globe artichoke	Fertile well-drained soil	A member of the thistle family, globe artichokes come in several varieties. To grow, the plant's deep root requires equally deep soil with sufficient space for root development.	Harvest by cutting the stem 2 to 3 inches below the base of the bud. Once the buds have been harvested, remove old stems to allow for new ones.

		Start the seeds indoors for about 4-8 weeks.	
		Transplant to the garden in a shady spot.	
		Plant the seeds ¼ inch deep in the soil and 3 feet apart in rows and water regularly. Shade from extremely hot noon sun.	
		They thrive when fertilized so try achieving the same effect with organic manure especially before planting and a little after.	
		Artichokes are susceptible to root	

		rot, therefore avoid overly wetting the soil.	
Green onions	Nutrient-rich soil	Instead of tossing the root of green onions/spring onions, you can regrow the roots. It's easy, simply slice off the ends of the bulbs and leave the roots still attached. Stand the bulbs with the ends down in a small jar. Add enough water to cover the roots and place on the windowsill. Ensure the roots stay moist and within a few days, green shoots will	As it grows, snip off the quantity you need. The green onions will continue to grow in the ground even after the ones in the pot dies off.

		appear on the bulbs. It grows really fast after that. Plant in your prepared garden or pot once the shoots are about 5 inches tall.	
Prickly pear	Well-draining decently fertile soil	One of the most undemanding plants you can grow in your summer garden, prickly pear is packed with nutrients. Planting is easy, select and split a ripe red fruit. Sprinkle the seeds in the pot or garden.	Prickly pear becomes fully mature around 12 – 30 inches tall

		Water if the soil feels dry. You can also plant from the cuttings	
		Cut off a single pad and allow its cut end to dry and heal for about a week.	
		Plant the pad with the cut end about 2 inches deep in the soil and water sparingly in dry soil.	
		It should take root in about a week.	
		Prickly pear is a cactus so you want to be careful when planting.	
		With it, garden safety gears like tweezers, kitchen	

		tongs and gloves are necessary.	
Rosemary	Well-drained fertile soil	This herb popularly used as a seasoning will make a great addition to your summer garden. Start the seeds by planting indoors for 7 to 10 before moving to the garden. As the herb grows relatively tall compared to most veggies, you should create enough room for it. Prune frequently so it doesn't become gangly.	For the freshest taste, harvest young stems and leaves. Allow the plants replace its growth before snipping more. You can also cut, dry and store the leaves in an airtight jar.

Sage	Fertile well-drained soil	This easy to grow herb is also popular as a seasoning for many food types. The pretty perennial herb needs full sun and well-drained soil to do well. This makes it an excellent summer crop. Sow the seeds up to two weeks indoors and transfer to the garden. At that point, the plant should be around 12 to 13 inches in height. You can plant near crops like carrot,	For the plant to reach its full potential, harvest lightly in the first year. After the first year, leave some stalks so it can regenerate.

| | | cabbage, and rosemary.

Ensure they don't lack moisture by watering regularly till they mature. | |
|---|---|---|---|
| **Broccoli rabe** | Well-drained soil rich in nutrients | Rich in vitamins and antioxidants, broccoli rabe is easy to grow.

Plant the seeds in the prepared garden.

In two or three days, it should germinate with the right soil and care.

Ensure they are adequately spaced so they quickly | Snip off the required quantity.

This is a cut and come again veggie; the harvest goes on for weeks. |

| | | grow into healthy leafy plants.

Cut off the first bud-bearing stem to aid the development and growth of multiple shoots. | |
|---|---|---|---|
| **Dill** | Well drained loamy soil with organic manure | Standing two feet tall at maturity, dill is an excellent summer crop.

Even in poor soil condition it grows. For a great harvest, a well-drained soil with a soil pH of 5.8 – 6.5 is essential.

Plant dill seeds directly on the ground about ¾ to 1 inches deep and | About 90 days after seeding, it should be matured enough for harvest. Cut close to the stem late evenings or early mornings.

The seeds become available for cutting once it blooms.

Cut two weeks after bloom and pack the cutting |

		13 – 15 inches apart.	in a paper bag after it dries.
Butter beans	Fertile soil amended with compost	Butter beans come in many varieties such as **Henderson, FordHook, Eastland** and **Thorogreen.** Planting them is easy and they do well in summer with the right care. Plant seeds 1 inch deep spacing 7-11 inches. Cover and water adequately. In a week or two, the sprouts should appear.	Butter beans are ready for harvest when the pods become plump with the beans. At this point, they are still bright green in color.

		Because butter beans do not perform well in dry soil, supply them with water regularly but don't flood them.	
Purple beans	Well-drained loamy soil	To plant purple beans, soak the seeds overnight in a bowl of cool water to aid sprouting. Dig rows 15 – 30 inches apart. Plant beans in 1inch trench and 2 inches apart. Cover the seeds. Water regularly but in moderation. To ensure a steady supply, plant extra	They're ready for harvest at about the same time as green beans.

		rows of beans every two weeks until the end of summer. Avoid high nitrogen fertilizers with this bean; else, you may end up with more leaves than beans.	
Thyme	Fertile soil, well-drained soil	What better time to grow this sweet-smelling plant than summer? It comes in many varieties and planting is easy. It is even easier to propagate from the cuttings than the seed. Cut about 3 inch from a stem and stick in a fertile soil, well-drained soil.	Thyme is best harvested before it flowers if you're looking to enjoy its potent flavor. The more you take snips from it, the more it grows. Cut in the morning, leaving the woody portions behind. Also, leave behind at least 5

| | | Roots should emerge in about 6 weeks.

Space seeds between 15 – 30 inches apart, depending on the variety. | inches of growth for regeneration. |
|---|---|---|---|
| **Dandelions** | Decently fertile soil | While many people see dandelions as weed to be eliminated when they appear, they are highly nutritious plants.

Plant the seeds in a shade to reduce their bitter taste and water regularly (this would also help reduce bitterness)

You can also reduce their bitterness by harvesting early. | They can be harvested by removing the entire plant or picking just the young leaves.

The choice is yours! |

• 20 Crops You Can Plant In Autumn

Just like winter, spring, and summer, crops can still thrive in the fall months. Once you know how to take advantage of the season's cooler temperature, rainfalls, and plant the right crops, your gardening season can be extended successfully.

In this section, we've listed out a number of crops suitable for planting in autumn, and a quick guide for planting them successfully.

Plant	Soil	Planting Instructions	Harvest time
Strawberries	Fertile loamy soil	While the plant is commonly sold for spring planting, it can still be bought for planting in autumn. To start, select only disease-resistant strains from a good nursery.	Strawberries are ready for harvest 4-6 weeks after blossoming. To harvest, pluck carefully to avoid destroying the plants and this should be done every 3 days.

		Roots should not be more than 8 inches long when you're set to plant.	
		Because strawberry spreads, create enough space for that by setting the plants 20 inches apart and 4 feet between the rows.	
		Prevent strawberry plants from fruiting in the first year by picking off their blossoms.	
		That way, their nutrient	

		reserves is spent in developing healthy roots thus making the yield greater in the second year.	
		Note also that the roots are shallow and as such, moisture is highly required when the runners and flowers begin to emerge.	
		Fight weed by removing as soon as you find them especially in the first few months of planting.	
		You can also protect blossoms and fruits from birds and other pests	

		by covering with row covers.	
Beet greens	Fertile garden soil	Get a bunch of beets, trim the top leaving about ½ inch of beet roots. Set the cut side down in a bowl of water and leave in a sunny area in your house.	In a week or less, beet greens should grow out. You can pick some then and leave the rest to mature more.
Chives	Well-drained loamy soil	Chives are easy to grow. Start indoors for up to four weeks. Then transfer to the prepared soil in the garden.	Chives are ready to be used 30 days after transplanting. Cut 2 inches down from the base to enjoy up to 4 harvests for the year.

Horseradish	Well-watered nutrient-rich loamy soil.	As a plant that thrives in almost any condition, horseradish truly deserves a place in your autumn kitchen. To plant this perennial in autumn, get the roots, (it's hard to find the seeds), cut off the top third to half of the root. The bottom part is what you should plant. Prepare the soil and mix with some organic manure.	Horseradish can be harvested one year after planting Loosen the soil carefully with a garden fork and remove.

		Plant the root 2 inches beneath the soil line. You can plant as much as two plants but usually, one plant would do for a family but don't forget to space out if you do plant more than one.	
Lamb lettuce	Fertile loamy soil	Lamb lettuce is a slow growing vegetable, so if you're including it in your autumn garden, you should successively sow large areas with the seeds for a reasonable harvest.	During harvest, lamb lettuce can be picked as whole or the leaves plucked separately.

		Plant the seed an inch deep into already prepared fertile soil. Water regularly and use cloches if you want, to speed up growth. But ensure they are open on very hot days as extreme heat could stunt their growth.	
Winter cress	Loamy, nutrient rich soil	Also known as the yellow rocket plant, winter cress belongs in the mustard family.	As it matures, pluck as much as you need by the stem.

		Growing it is easy. Plant the seeds in prepared fertile soil. Provide regularly with water in dry weather but don't flood it.	
Lemongrass	Fertile well-draining soil	This sweet-smelling plant does well in autumn. Buy the plant and trim about 5cm off the top of the plant. Place the stalk in a bowl of water and place in a sunny spot in your home,	On average, lemongrass will be ready for harvest in about 85 – 100 days. Gently pull out the quantity you need and leave the rest watered.

		In a few weeks, the roots should appear at the stalk.	
		At that point, transfer to a prepared pot or garden with fertile soil.	
		Water regularly.	
Chinese broccoli	Well-drained nutrient-rich soil	With minimal care, this nutrient-rich vegetable does well in winter.	Chinese broccoli should be ready for harvest in about 60 – 70 days.
		Sow the seeds in fertile prepared soil spaced 1 inch apart and rows 18 inches apart.	Harvest the fresh stems and leaves when the first flowers emerge.

| | | Seeds should sprout in 10 – 15 days.

Once they are about 3 inches tall, the plants should be thinned 8inches apart. | For a longer harvest, pluck the stalk 8 inches from the top with a sharp knife. |
|---|---|---|---|
| **Celery** | Compost-rich moisture retentive soil | A cool weather crop that thrives in autumn, celery is one plant you certainly want to include in your autumn garden.

It is rich in nutrients and easy to grow. It flourishes on a | Your plants should be ready for harvest within 100 – 120 days from transplant.

You can harvest by cutting off at the head or a little below the soil level. |

		pH between 5.8 – 6.8	
		Start the seeds indoors for about 8 -10 weeks and transplant to your already prepared compost-rich garden.	
		Sow the seeds about ½ inch deep and 6 – 10 inches apart.	
		Keep the plants well watered at all stages of growth as lack of water could stunt their growth and cause stringiness.	

| Cucamelons | Well-drained nutrient-rich soil | A distant relative of cucumbers, cucamelons are easy to grow as they are rarely troubled by common garden pests.

Planting the nutritious melon is easy and the vines exceptionally productive.

Start the seeds indoors 6 weeks before you plant.

Sow in 4 inch pots so plants get a chance to develop a solid root system before | Begin to check for ripe cucamelons about 7 days after you spot the flowers.

You want to start picking when they are young as tanginess increases as they age. |

		transplanting to the garden.	
		Soil must be rich and well-drained for these melons to perform well.	
		As they grow, support the plant with trellises to keep foliage off the ground and greatly reduce the risk of diseases.	
Warrigal greens	Fertile well-drained soil	Also known as Botany Bay Spinach or Sea Spinach, this nutrient-rich vegetable thrives in well-drained fertile soil.	The seeds of the warrigal grow for a long time even after your first harvest.

		It can be grown from its cuttings or the seeds directly on the soil.	Take only the quantity you need at a time and try not to step on them while at it.
		Keep watered once planted. They do not need any special nutrients, just a good healthy soil, sunlight, and water.	
Mushrooms	Well-drained potted soil	While growing mushrooms is a lot different from growing most other crops, it can still be organically grown in your home.	Mushrooms should emerge within three to four weeks. Harvest once the cap opens. It can be snipped from

		Yes, with the right conditions mushrooms will grow.	the stalk with a sharp knife.
			Harvest every day or as needed.
		There are several kinds of mushrooms you can plant each with its specific needs.	
		To grow indoors, you'll need a couple of materials that can ease things for you.	
		There are many mushroom kits packed with a growing medium already inoculated with the spawn.	

		Fill trays with mushroom compost materials and inoculate with spawn.	
		Raise the temperature to around 70 degrees F for up to 21 days or till the mycelium begin to appear.	
		Drop temperatures to 55 to 60 degrees F.	
		Cover the spawn with an inch of potting soil and keep the soil is kept moist by spritzing with a damp cloth.	

Maruba Santoh	Fertile well-drained soil	The mild-tasting Maruba Santoh is easy to plant and grows quickly. A loose head type Chinese cabbage, the plant has smooth light green tender leaves and white petioles. It can also be harvested at any stage. Because it does better in cool temperatures, the winter weather is perfect for it.	Maruba Santoh is ready for harvest within 30 – 40 days after planting.

		Sow seeds in fertile well-drained soil.	
Water pepper	Fertile well-drained soil	This annual plant is easy to grow. You can soak the seeds in cold water for a few days to boost their germination rate. It enjoys sunlight and moisture so plant in a spot in your garden with direct sunlight and regularly supply with water.	It is ready for harvest once it turns red.
Chinese celery	Nutrient rich loamy soil	Chinese celery is easy to grow especially in the	The leaves can be harvest when they're

		cool autumn weather.	about 20-30 cm tall.
		Get the bases and press them into fertile loamy soil in a pot or garden.	
		The leaves should begin to grow in a day or two.	
Roselle	Rich loamy soil	The stunning red color Roselle plant will not only add beauty to your garden, it is high in nutrients as well.	The calyxes are ready for harvest when fully grown but still tender.
		It is fast growing and easy to grow.	
		Start them in a pot and transplant them to the garden	

		when they're about 3 – 4cm tall.	
		Allow about 5 feet spaces in rows and the plants 3 feet apart.	
		Supply with water regularly.	
Lemon	Well-drained slightly acidic soil	Growing lemons isn't as hard as many think.	Lemon tree starts to fruit between two to three years.
		Dig a hole a bit shallower than the root length and replace soil.	If well-cared for, the reward is always worth the wait.
		Water adequately and regularly and mulch if you can as they	

		require it to flourish. You can also prune to maintain their shape and height. They require a lot of light so plant them in strategic spots in the garden.	
Chrysanthe mum	Fertile loamy soil	A member of the daisy family, chrysanthemum adds a distinct taste to soups and stir fries. The leaves when young can be enjoyed in stir-fries while the edible flower petals	In 5 to 6 weeks, chrysanthemum is ready to be harvested.

| | | can be added to salads.

Autumn remains one of the best time of the year to plant it.

Plant seeds 1 inch deep and space 15cm apart in nutrient rich soil. | |
|---|---|---|---|
| **Burdock** | Well-drained rich loamy soil | A plant prized for its medicinal properties, burdock thrives in the cool autumn months.

Start seeds in a tray or directly in the garden | Burdock is usually ready for harvest 10 weeks after planting but you can leave it to mature more in the soil if you want. |

		while you prepare the soil and enrich with organic manure.	
		Move the seedlings to their final location in a soil with a pH around 6.6 – 7.5.	
		Provide up to 20cm spacing between them.	
		Burdocks can't be grown in pots because of their deep roots.	
		Water regularly but don't flood or keep it waterlogged.	

		Remove weeds competing for nutrients.	
Bergamot	Fertile garden soil	This plant grows well in cool autumn months. Start the seeds indoors and transfer to the garden. Transplant 18inches apart as they spread easily. Include mulch if you want and water regularly.	Collect leaves as they mature. The flowers can be picked when opened.

• 20 Other Herbs and Spices for All Seasons

Below you'll find a number of herbs and a rundown of how they can be planted. So, whether you're looking to grow herbs as a hobby, save money or just want to enjoy herbs as fresh as possible, you'll find most of the popular herbs here.

The best part? They grow in all seasons with the right soil and care! Read on.

Plant	Soil	Planting Instructions	Harvest time
Bay leaves	Normal garden soil	Bay leaves make fantastic additions to every garden. Planting may be a little challenging but can be done.	Bay leaves can be enjoyed dried or fresh though fresh ones are stronger in flavor than dried ones.

		Lacerate your seeds and plant them in a container or pot, then cover. . It can take between 5 – 12 months to germinate and it should be kept in the container or pot for about 2 years before moving to the garden. Water regularly especially in summer and add compost for nutrients.	And they're available all year round.
Yarrow	Decently fertile soil	Like dandelion, many view this plant as just a weed. How wrong!	The leaves can be harvested when they start growing.

			The flowers on the other hand can be harvested when fully open.
		They're highly medicinal and worth having in any garden. Start the seeds indoors then move outdoors after 6 weeks. Because the plant can be invasive, you'll need to space after some weeks and discard the extras.	
Lemon Verbena	Loose, well-drained soil rich in organic matter	To grow in a container this sweet-smelling, choose a container about 12 inches wide so it gets enough space to spread.	Harvest as needed during its growth. Cooking tip: to release the sweet lemon flavor, crush

		You can provide insulation for the roots by burying the pot/container in the ground particularly in cold weather. Ensure it is provide with organic matter to aid its growth. Remember to move plants indoors when the drops excessively. Watch out for mites and whiteflies as they're commonly around this plant.	leaves before use.
Tarragon	Well-drained loamy soil	With its slight anise flavor, this herb grows well in almost every season.	To harvest tarragon, snip the light green leaves and don't harvest over 1/3 of the

		However, it requires extra care throughout planting as it is delicate but the reward is worth it.	plant at a time as it could weaken or even kill it.
		There are several varieties of this plant but the French tarragon is probably one of the most popular.	
		The plants thrive in a soil pH of 6.5 – 7.5	
		Plant the seeds one inch deep in the soil with plenty of space to spread.	
		Also avoid planting invasive herbs such as	

		oregano near to avoid choking it. Moderately supply with water. They should germinate in about 10 to 14 days. Prune as often as possible.	
Oregano	Well-drained sandy loam soil with compost	Oreganos come in many different species. Generally however, they prefer a pH around 6.0 – 8.0. You can lower soil acidity if you need to by placing wood ashes around the plants in winter. Plant the seeds on recently turned soil	Pruning goes hand in hand with harvesting. Prune and use to allow for more growth.

		and tap into place. Sprinkle with some dampened soil. Check for weeds regularly, prune, and water the soil when dry.	
Sweet Marjoram	Well-drained decently fertile soil	This plant can grow as high as 10 to 20 inches tall. To plant, sow the seeds ¼ inch deep and thin later to 7 inches apart. Rows should be spaced 16 – 22 inches apart. Until it is established, marjoram needs regular water supply to thrive.	Marjoram is set for harvest 60 days after it is planted. Harvest moderately so it grows more.

Stevia	Well-drained fertile soil	The sweet plant is easy to grow in well-drained beds or even large containers. It grows excellently warm weather and with the right conditions it can grow up to 24 inches tall and wide. Start indoors for a few weeks and move the seedlings to the garden. Space 2 feet apart in accessible areas of your garden.	Stevia can be harvested by cutting back the leaves about half their sizes. It can also be dried after harvest and stored in a cool, dry container.
Chervil	Nutrient-rich loam soil	A member of the carrot family, chervil can grow up to two feet tall.	The plant reaches maturity in about 40 – 60 days.

		The parsley lookalike is not very easy to find so growing it yourself may be your best option. To grow chervil from seed, plant the fresh seeds in a fertile soil and space 6inches to a foot apart. Seeds should germinate in a week or two.	You can harvest as much as you need then.
Milk thistle	Rich well-drained soil	Famed for its medicinal property, this plant surely deserves a place in your herb garden.	Milk thistle is ready for harvest once mature.

		Plant 1/3 inch deep spacing 16 – 36 inches. The plant needs sunlight to do well so plant in a good location in your garden. It should germinate within 2 – 4 weeks after planting. It doesn't need as much water as most herbs.	
Licorice	Sandy moist soil	The licorice plant offers you so many health benefits plus growing it is easy. It can be grown from seeds or the rhizome as long as	The roots of the licorice can be harvested after about three years. To harvest, loosen the

		it still has a bud on it. You can start seeds indoors in autumn transplant to the garden in spring. Within 14 – 20 days, it should germinate. Thin to about 12 – 36 inches apart.	soil with a garden fork and pull the roots out.
Ginger	Fertile loamy soil	Ginger roots are found in every grocery store but if you intend to grow at home, it's easy to do. Pick a healthy plump ginger about 4 – 5 inches long with some "fingers".	In 10 months, ginger should be mature enough for harvest.

		Plant about 1 inch deep in the soil. Water regularly and thoroughly. You should see leaves in a week or two.	
Aloe Vera	Well-drained soil	Aloe can do well in any weather when grown right but requires minimal effort in warm weather. Get a healthy aloe plant and prepare the soil in a pot with proper drainage holes beneath them to drain out excess water. For this, you should opt for	Harvest as much as you need when mature and continue watering the rest.

		terracotta, plastics, or ceramics.	
		Take a leaf from the aloe plant, tear from the plant till the center and place over your prepared soil.	
		Push in a bit with half the plant exposed to light.	
		Place a tray at the pot's bottom to hold excessive water draining out from holes.	
		Water frequently but let the excess water drain out.	

Fennel	Fertile loamy soil	Possibly one of the most agreeable garden plants, growing fennel is simple.	Fennel begins to flower 90 days after planting.
		Soak seeds 24hrs before to aid germination. Choose a sunny location in a well-drained garden soil and plant the seeds about an inch deep.	It can be harvested from that time though blooms best in the second year.
		Water regularly and in the second year, it should bloom adequately and even make a good backdrop for many other plants.	
		Fennel does well in an acidic soil and organic matter can	

		be used to boost soil fertility.	
German Chamomile	Well-drained soil	This highly medicinal plant requires light to thrive. Start indoors for a few weeks and move to the garden on a soil with a pH between 5.6 – 7.5 You can also plant directly once all risk of frost has passed. They become very hardy once they take roots. Water regularly and keep your eyes open for pests such as aphids and mealybugs.	Chamomiles can be harvested once they grow to a height of about 20 – 30 inches.
Turmeric	Fertile garden soil	Just like ginger, turmeric grows a rhizome	Turmeric is ready for harvest

		(underground tuber)	within 8 – 10 months.
		Buy fresh turmeric roots and plant an inch deep spacing each 12 – 16 inches apart in a fertile soil enriched with organic matter. Water regularly and keep out pests.	The leaves should begin to dry out. Take out the amount you need without having to dig out entire soil.
Sorrel	Fertile well-drained soil	A green leafy vegetable, it is grown for its tart lemon flavor. It prefers the cool fall and spring seasons but would still grow with the right care in other months.	To fully mature, the plant need about 50 – 60 days and can be harvested when there are up to four inches long.

		Plant in spot with acidity around 5.5 to 6.8.	
		Also supply the soil with organic matter for the leaves to do well.	
		Sow seeds 1 inch deep and space 3 inches apart.	
		Thin later to about 12 – 15 inches spacing.	
		Sorrel needs water to flourish so supply with water frequently.	
		It is not usually disturbed by pests	

		except aphid sometimes. Rinse off with water if you see them.	
Caraway	Fertile loamy soil with compost	An aromatic herb, caraway can grow about 30 inches tall. Plant the seeds in a fertile well-drained soil with a pH around 6.5 to 7.0. Sow about ½ inch deep. This plant enjoys the cool fall and spring weather but will grow in the rest months with the right care. Thin the seeds to 7- 12 inches apart	All the parts of the caraway plants are edible. And from the second or even the first year, the leaves can be harvest for used in salads and stir-fries. The seeds are also mature for harvest when they

		once they germinate, and mulch with straw or organic mulch for additional nutrients.	turn deep brown.
Anise plant	Nutrient-rich loamy soil	The anise plants are grown for their seeds. To grow successfully, they need a moderately alkaline soil pH of 6.3 – 7.0, full sun, and a well-drained soil. They also require regular supply of water until well-established. Plant the seeds ½ inch deep and space 2 to 3 feet apart. Water the plants twice weekly at	Anise is mature for harvest in about 120 – 140 days. Harvest as needed, and then store the extras for future use.

		least until they're 6 – 8 inches tall. You can apply organic matter prior to flowering.	
Catnip	Moderately-rich well-drained soil	Grown easily by the seeds, stem cuttings and roots, it is popular for its cat-attracting qualities. Humans also benefit from its medicinal qualities. Too grow, start the seeds in containers for some weeks and then move to a prepared garden with a pH between 6.1 to 7.8 In the garden, space about 15 to 18 inches apart.	At maturity, catnips grow to a height of 3 to 4 feet. Remove the flowers if you're not looking to get volunteer seedlings the next season.

		Water regularly and add some compost manure.	
Mints	Nutrient rich garden soil	Mints are slow-growing plants. So, plant indoors for about 6 weeks before moving to the garden. Or purchase the mint seedling from the nursery and then transplant to the soil. Mint doesn't do very well with too much sun so keep it in a place where it receives it mildly. You also want to give it ample space to grow as it runs through the soil easily.	It takes about 85 to 90 days to maturity. By then, it would have achieved its complete height of about 1 to 2 feet and ready for harvest. In a few weeks, it should grow again to harvest height.

There you go; 100 plants you can cultivate in your garden in any weather. While most have been categorized under each of the four seasons, they can still be grown in almost any season or weather.

You just have to ensure extra care is taken with such and the required nutrients are supplied. That way, you're never out of your favorite vegetable, fruit or herb. Also, trellises, row covers, and a nutrient-dense soil are just as important as the plants.

Use them when required; they make can make all the difference between a good harvest and a fantastic one.

CHAPTER 10
HOW TO STORE YOUR CROPS

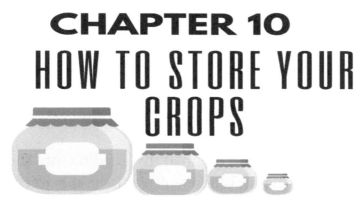

If you follow the right procedure of garden preparation, planting, watering, fertilizing, and pest control, then you should have a bumper harvest at the end of the season. And since you can't hope to eat everything garden fresh (however awesome that would be), you will have to learn how to preserve your crops. Below are 10 methods of preservation for different types of vegetables.

• <u>Methods of vegetable preservation</u>

1. Freezing

Extreme cold has the effect of slowing down bodily functions in all living organisms, including the microorganisms that cause food to go bad. It is possible to extend the lifespan of vegetables like kales, spinach, cucumbers among numerous others by a few weeks by simply storing them in the freezer. However, you can extend the storage time by first blanching (dipping in hot water for a few seconds) before placing them in freezer bags and into the fridge. The good thing about frozen foods is that they retain some of their farm freshness even when you take them out of the fridge a few months after harvesting.

2. Drying

Microorganisms make food go bad by feeding on the nutritious juices in them. When you remove the juices from food, what remains can stay around for much longer without going bad. That is why dried grains can last years without developing mold-based infections. A food dehydrator comes in handy for drying vegetables like tomatoes, sucking away all the moisture and leaving behind a dry tomato that can remain edible for much, much longer even though it loses the farm-freshness.

3. Jellying

Making jelly is not only a very effective method of

preserving vegetables, but it is also a recipe for nice meals that you can enjoy snacking on or adding   food for a very long time. Preserving by jellying can either produce jellies or jams. With jellies, seeds are removed very diligently to leave a very consistent blend while jams leave the seeds in for a healthier, more wholesome blend. The process of jellying does not really preserve foods in its own right. Instead, it makes those tomatoes, watermelons, or pumpkins easier to store in a freezer where they can last longer as jellies than as whole fruits.

4. Dark storage

Dark storage or root cellar is a method of preservation very specific to root vegetables like potatoes, sweet potatoes, and carrots. Preparation for storage may involve washing with a light spray of water to remove garden dirt, but the skin should not be bruised, otherwise the root tuber might develop fungal infections. Tomatoes can also be stored in a dark room, but they need to be unripe and be packed in a very light manner to avoid bruising and resultant rot.

5. Pickling

Some vegetables preserve very well when stored in a jar containing a boiled mixture of vinegar and sugar. The sugar/vinegar solution is very effective as a preservative, prolonging the life of your vegetable and giving you an infinite source of delicious snacks and veggies to put in your hamburgers to make them that much healthier. Some of the best vegetables to pickle include radishes, jalapenos, and cucumbers.

6. Salting

A salt solution creates a very inhospitable environment for microorganisms by removing the water in the vegetable. Storing vegetables in a jar containing a salt solution preserves their edibility and seasons them at the same time too.

7. Alcohol immersion

This is another method of preservation that works by extracting water from the vegetable to prevent the development of microbes. The vegetables should be sliced up and completely submerged in the alcohol for this method of preservation to work. The larger the surface area of the vegetable exposed to alcohol, the more the water that will be drawn out and thus the more effective the preservation will be.

8. Vacuum sealing

Vacuum sealing is a relatively easy method of vegetable preservation. It requires that you first place your food in a freezer, and then put them in airtight bags that have been emptied of all air, seal, and store it. The lack of air inhibits the growth of microorganisms and allows your food to last a long time.

9. Canning

Canning is the most effective method of storing vegetables. The method is easy enough that it is possible to can anything. It is also outstanding in that it entails the storage of fully cooked meals which are then stored in a safe and healthy way until you need to eat it. Say you like eating mashed potatoes and your garden just produced a healthy yield of potatoes, you simply mash them, store them in a sterilized jar and close it up. Any time you feel like having a dish of mashed potatoes, you simply open a can and enjoy! Not only is canning easy and uncomplicated, it is also safer than other methods of preservation. And what's more, it allows you to preserve a meal instead of just an ingredient to a great meal in the future.

10.Sugar

Sugar is great for preserving vegetables (and generally foods) with their own natural sugars. Sugaring involves dipping your watermelon or cucumber in a sugar solution and crystallizing, forming a protective coat that doubles up as a treat for future snacking.

- ## Example recipe

You might be thinking that the methods listed above sound very complicated, but they are really quite simple. In fact, you'd be surprised to find out how easy it is to make gourmet-quality condiments right from your vegetable garden.

Giardiniera

Giardiniera is an Italian entrée made from carrots, peppers, cauliflower, and a bunch of other vegetables. It adds some measure of sophistication   to your mealtimes and also provides a very healthy vegetable side dish. The recipe given below is derived from the kitchens of Home Taste Kitchen from Milwaukee, Wisconsin.

It has a preparation time of 1 hour and makes 10 pints of canned greatness. A cup is used as a measure of volume equal to one-   sixteenth of a gallon.

Ingredients

Six cups of white vinegar

Three and a half of sugar

Three cups of water

Four and a half teaspoonful of salt

A tablespoonful of oregano

A tablespoonful of fennels

Twelve cups of cauliflower (the equivalence of about two heads of cauliflower)

Four carrots

Four celery sticks in half-inch cuts

Forty eight pearl onions

Four big red peppers in half-inch slices

Four seedless Serrano peppers

Ten bay leaves

20 peppercorns, and

Ten garlic cloves

Directions

1. Pour the water, vinegar, and sugar into a big pot.

2. Add your salt, fennel seeds, and oregano then boil.

3. Throw in your celery, onions (chopped), cauliflower, and carrots and boil the mixture again.

4. Turn off your heat and add red peppers.

Your entrée is ready for preservation by canning.

1. Take your ten one-pint jars and fill them up with the mixture, taking care to leave a space of about half an inch from filling capacity.

2. Add 2 peppercorns, a few slices of garlic, and a bay leaf in every jar.

3. Drive out any air bubbles from the jars and wipe the rim to ensure that the lids fit perfectly.

4. Screw the lids on just tight enough.

5. Immerse the jars in a canner half-full of boiling water and leave them in there for 10 minutes

Once cooled, your condiment can be stored for up to three months in perfect condition.

References

Mannelly, T. (2017). 10 reasons to start a garden. *Oh Lardy!* Retrieved from https://ohlardy.com/ on 6 May 2019

Frost, S. (2018). The disadvantages of planting a garden. *SFGate Home Guides.* Retrieved from https://www.sfgate.com/ on 6 May 2019

Masabni, J. (2019). Planning a garden. *Texas A&M Agrilife Extension.* Retrieved from https://agrilifeextension.tamu.edu/ on 6 May 2019

Tilley, N. (2016). Growing a vertical vegetable garden. *Gardening Know How.* Retrieved from https://www.gardeningknowhow.com/ on 6 May 2019

Lipford, D. (n.d.). Choosing the right size vegetable garden. *Today's Homeowner.* Retrieved from https://www.todayshomeowner.com/ on 6 May 2019

Seaman, G. (2014). 5 easy ways to assess your soil for gardening. *Eartheasy Sustainable Living.* Retrieved from https://eartheasy.com/ on 6 May 2019

Barton, R. (2013). Know your garden soil: How to make the most of your soil type. *Eartheasy Sustainable Living.* Retrieved from https://eartheasy.com/ on 6 May 2019

Gardener's Supply (2019).The Basics: Gardening in raised beds. *Gardener's Supply Company.* Retrieved from https://www.gardeners.com/ on 6 May 2019

Gilsenan, F., & Lindsey, J. (2019). How to build a raised garden bed. *Popular Mechanics.* Retrieved from https://www.popularmechanics.com/ on 6 May 2019

Countryfarm Lifestyles (2019). 12 essential garden tools no gardener should be without! *Countryfarm Lifestyles.* Retrieved from http://www.countryfarm-lifestyles.com/ on 6 May 2019

The RBKC (2019). Which plants should I be planting and when? *The Royal Borough of Kensington and Chelsea.* Retrieved from https://www.rbkc.gov.uk/ on 6 May 2019

Cruciferous vegetables list & how to grow them. *Backyard Garden Lover.* Retrieved from https://www.backyardgardenlover.com/ on 6 May 2019

Benjamin, B. (2019). Beth's guide for growing the cucurbit family: Cucumbers, summer & winter squashes, melons & gourds. *Renee's Garden.* Retrieved from https://www.reneesgarden.com/ on 6 May 2019

Gardening Channel (2019). Root crops for the home garden. *Gardening Channel.* Retrieved from https://www.gardeningchannel.com/ on 6 May 2019

How to grow allium vegetables. *Backyard Garden Lover.* Retrieved from https://www.backyardgardenlover.com/ on 6 May 2019

Masabini, J. (2018). Fertilizing a garden. *Texas A&M Agrilife Extension.* Retrieved from https://agrilifeextension.tamu.edu/ on 6 May 2019

Gazeley, H. (2013). Earthworms- An essential part of any vegetable garden. *Growing Interactive Ltd.* Retrieved from https://www.growveg.com/ on 6 May 2019

The Editors (2018). The 10 most destructive garden insects and how to get rid of them. *Good Housekeeping*. Retrieved from https://www.goodhousekeeping.com/ on 6 May 2019

Eartheasy (2019). Natural garden pest control. *Eartheasy Sustainable Living*. Retrieved from https://eartheasy.com/ on 6 May 2019

Oder, T. (2016). Are you watering your veggies the right way? *Mother Nature Network*. Retrieved from https://www.mnn.com/ on 6 May 2019

Poindexter, J. (2019). 12 food preservation methods to make your food & harvest last longer. *Morningchores*. Retrieved from https://morningchores.com/ on 6 May 2019

Taste of Home Test Kitchen (2019). Giardiniera. *Taste of Home*. Retrieved from https://www.tasteofhome.com/ on 13 May 2019

Index: 100 Vegetables

THANK YOU!

**YOU CAN NOW
ACCESS OUR
EXCLUSIVE FACEBOOK
COMMUNITY..**

**SHARE YOUR THOUGHTS,
ASK QUESTIONS AND
INTERACT WITH FELLOW
GARDENERS ANYTIME!**

**JUST CLICK THE LINK
BELOW..**

**SHARE YOUR THOUGHTS,
ASK QUESTIONS AND
INTERACT WITH FELLOW
GARDENERS ANYTIME!**

**JUST CLICK THE LINK
BELOW..**

http://bit.ly/2wFqptD

**Get your free E-book version of this
book**

Follow the link or scan the QR code

https://bit.ly/3Y3oDwP

Made in United States
Troutdale, OR
01/26/2024

17180483R00130